SPIES IN DISGUISE AT GETTYSBURG

by Mary Morgan

Enjoy the adventure - Mary Morgan

Illustrated by Dawn McVay Baumer

978-0-9891462-2-7

Gettysburg is a product of the imagination of the author. None of the events described in this story occurred. This story has no purpose other than to entertain and educate the reader. Names of all characters and photographs in the book are used with permission.

Printed in the USA.

Manufactured by Color House Graphics, Inc., Grand Rapids, MI USA
September 2014
Job #43963

Published by Buttonwood Press, LLC
P.O. Box 716, Haslett, Michigan 48840
www.buttonwoodpress.com

Bryon and Shannon Morgan – 1987

Acknowledgements

I would like to thank my husband, Randy, for his continual support in writing these national park mystery stories, and my children, Shannon and Bryon, who traveled with us, getting a history lesson during our summer vacations.

Many thanks to the Buttonwood Press staff for their combined efforts to publish this book in time for the 150th anniversary celebration at Gettysburg —July 2013.

Thank you to my technical support—Brenda, John, Shannon, Chris, Pam, Laurie, Judy, my dad Wayne Price, who taught me how to play Marbles, and my friend Leon (Barney) Farnsworth great-great-great-cousin of General Elon Farnsworth, who shared family stories of Gettysburg.

Thanks to the kids in my life who are my characters: Hannah and Ethan Hopewell (the real Ben and Bekka) and Stephen Hartley.

The students from NY, PA, GA, SC, and VA are my nieces and nephews—Northern and Southern cousins. Thanks for lending me your names.

The town of Gettysburg and Civil War Battlefields

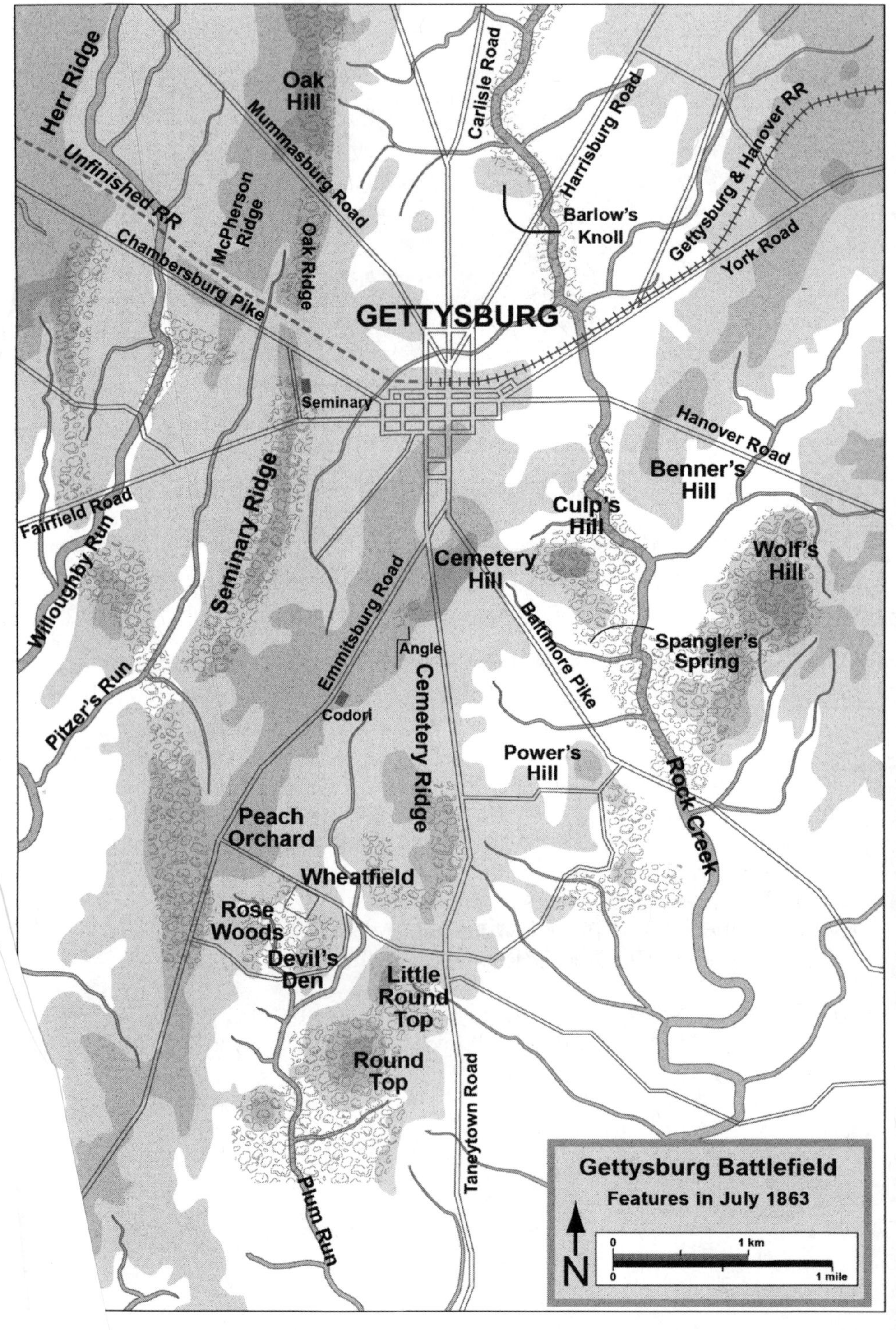

Dedication

This book is dedicated
to the memory of those who gave
their lives on the battlefields
for what they believed
to be right for our country.

Other National Park Mystery Books by Mary Morgan

Published by Buttonwood Press, LLC

Stolen Treasures at Pictured Rocks
© Mary Morgan, 2011
ISBN = 978-0-9823351-3-0

The Face at Mount Rushmore
© Mary Morgan, 2012
ISBN = 978-0-9823351-7-8

Snow Den at Yellowstone
© Mary Morgan, 2014
ISBN = 978-0-9891462-5-8

Double Trouble in the Everglades
© Mary Morgan, 2015
ISBN = 978-0-9965562-0-0

Twisted Trails in Grand Canyon
© Mary Morgan, 2016
ISBN = 978-0-9972464-4-5

To order books:

www.nationalparkmysteries.com

www.ButtonwoodPress.com

Chapter 1

"Ben Cooper."

"Here."

"Stephen Farnsworth."

"Here."

"You boys are staying in tent number thirteen," their teacher Mr. Dupries instructed, pointing to a row of old white canvas tents set up in the open field in Gettysburg Military National Park.

"Thirteen, isn't that unlucky?" Ben asked his friend, as he mentally counted where their tent was located.

"Yeah," Stephen said, grabbing his backpack. Looking around, he added, "But what can be unlucky here?"

"Well, we could burn down our tent with a lantern, get in the way of a cannonball, stab ourselves with a sword, or..."

"Okay, okay, you're right." Stephen's eyes bulged and his mouth grimaced as he thought of the possibilities.

"Watch yourself, there are snakes here too," Ben added. "My sister Bekka did one of her famous FYI readings just before we left home." Mocking her voice he said with a girly tone, "For Your Information, there are five kinds of snakes: garter and black rat snakes that are non-venomous, copperhead and timber

rattlesnakes that are poisonous, and the northern water snake that looks like it's poisonous, but isn't."

"Hey, you making fun of me, Ben?" a voice from behind them called. Busted!

Turning around, Ben came face to face with his twin sister Bekka, spelling bee champ and master informer of trivia. She really wasn't a bad sister. In fact, they were great pals most of the time. She wasn't too girly. In fact, she could climb the rope ladder in their maple tree and hang upside down just as well as he could. And she wasn't too annoying. In fact, she didn't say anything when he slept in his clothes and wore them again the next day. If he had to choose a sister out of all the girls he knew, he'd choose Bekka. But right now, she was in his face for mocking her FYIs—short for "For Your Information."

"Uh, no, I was just warning Stephen about the snakes you said are here." It was rather hard to keep a straight face.

Looking him right in the eye she stated, "Someday one of my FYIs just might save your—"

BOOM! A deafening sound behind them made all three kids jump and duck.

Stephen looked around, spotting the smoke rising from a cannon in a nearby field. "That was loud! I'm gonna go deaf if we have to hear that all week. I hope my ear drums survive."

Being chosen to go to Gettysburg Military National Park in Pennsylvania was a great honor, but having his ears blasted off

was something else. He hadn't thought to pack a pair of ear plugs. He didn't know he'd need them!

"If we go home deaf, it's your fault," Ben stated, hoping the ringing in his ears would quit.

Chapter 2

Of all the fifth grade classes in Michigan, their class in Lansing was the one chosen to go to Gettysburg, Pennsylvania, because Stephen won the essay contest. No one knew he was almost famous.

In January, their teacher Mr. Dupries announced there was a contest for all fifth grade students to write a five-hundred word essay on why they wanted to go to Gettysburg to attend a reenactment of the famous three-day Civil War battle. Their class studied the 1863 battle between the armies of the North and the South in Social Studies, and located Gettysburg on a map of Pennsylvania, but most couldn't come up with a winning reason why they would want to go there. Except Stephen.

It took him three days to write his five-hundred word essay, but when he turned it in, he didn't tell anyone what was on his paper. He just grinned.

Bekka wrote that she would like to go see what old army hospitals were like because she wanted to be a nurse. Ben thought it would be cool to see the cannons and guns. He liked artillery weapons. But neither were winning ideas.

Three months went by. Without an explanation, a special assembly at school was announced. All students had to be in the gym first thing on Friday morning. They tried to guess why. Everyone had forgotten about the essay contest.

Mrs. Ranes, their principal, asked for everyone to be quiet because she had a special announcement. Ben looked around at the adults standing by the wall—several had tags with TV Channel 10, Channel 6, Channel 53, and Fox 47 written on them. Wow, he thought, we're going to be on TV. Whatever is happening must be really special.

Bekka poked him as she pointed to one reporter. "Look, that's the man from TV. What's happening?"

"Students, please quiet down," Mrs. Ranes said into the microphone again. She was short, but she had a big voice. "I have a special announcement."

Everyone became quiet and listened as she told about the contest, and how someone from their school, of all fifth grade classes in Michigan, had written the winning essay. She further explained it meant the whole fifth grade class would be going to Gettysburg, Pennsylvania, for a special reenactment. Kids looked left and right and whispered who they thought it might be. Some of the fifth graders were sure they were the one. Excitement mounted. One girl got butterflies in her stomach just thinking about going up in front of everyone to get the prize. She hoped she didn't win.

Mrs. Ranes held up a white envelope which contained the winner's name. She waited for silence, looked around to be sure everyone was watching, and then began ripping it open. Slowly. The suspense was almost too much for the fifth grade class. Girls held hands and closed their eyes.

"The winner of the fifth grade contest, 'Why I Want to Go to Gettysburg,' is..."

She paused to make it more suspenseful. No one breathed or coughed or anything.

Finally, she said, "The winner is Stephen Farnsworth!"

"Stephen Farnsworth," echoed many voices. All eyes went to the section where the fifth grade class was sitting.

Stephen couldn't believe his ears. Ben high-fived him.

"Stephen, please come to the front and receive your official Gettysburg packet of information," Mrs. Ranes said cheerfully into the microphone.

Stephen stood up and climbed over other students as he made his way to the front. He was smiling big enough to show most of his teeth. Several cameras flashed, taking his picture. Everyone clapped and cheered. Ben and Bekka both wondered what he had written that was so special.

As he stood in front of the microphone, Mrs. Ranes asked him one question, "Stephen, why do you want to go to Gettysburg?"

Pointing to his fingers he began, "My great-great-great-great-great-great-great-great-great-grandfather, General Farnsworth marched from Detroit with his Army brigade and fought there."

A wave of "wow" rippled around the gym and then the clapping and cheering began all over again.

"And how do you know this is true?" Mrs. Ranes quizzed him.

"Because my grandmother looked it up in our family genie, genie, genie something book," he answered, forgetting how to pronounce the long word.

"It's a genealogy book, also known as a family history book," Mrs. Ranes said. "We did some fact-checking ourselves, and yes, your great-great-great—seven greats—grandfather was at Gettysburg, so all the judges felt it would be good for you to go see the place where he fought one hundred and fifty years ago."

Turning to the fifth grade, she stated, "Fifth grade students, you will leave in one month to be part of a re-enactment. At a reenactment, you live like the people lived back then, you'll wear clothes from that era, boys will wear Army clothes, you'll cook food outdoors, sleep in tents, play new games and make friends with people from the South. It's a once-in-a-lifetime experience which you'll remember forever. Thank you, Stephen, for being a greaaaat grandson to a famous Farnsworth. You're a winner in everybody's book."

Chapter 3

After school, Ben and Bekka could hardly wait to tell their parents the news. Mr. and Mrs. Cooper couldn't believe it when their kids told them they'd be gone six days with their school class. How would their hamster survive without Ben playing with him and how could they live with peace and quiet in the house? Was there a store where they could rent-a-kid for an afternoon? Just for a little noise.

Usually their family took trips together, but this time it was just three teachers and twenty students riding a bus to the national park in Gettysburg, Pennsylvania–five hundred miles away. Students from six states would be there. Three northern states: Michigan, New York, and Pennsylvania, and three southern states: Virginia, South Carolina, and Georgia. Some of Ben and Bekka's cousins lived in Pennsylvania and New York, and one of their classmates, Lajonte Jones, L.J. for short, had a cousin in Virginia, but no one knew anyone from South Carolina or Georgia.

Along with Mrs. Ranes and Mr. Dupries, Miss Iversen, their history teacher, was chosen to go. Miss Iversen made them check out library books about Gettysburg to see what kind of clothes they wore and what food they cooked on the battlefields.

Everyone went to costume shops to get old-fashioned clothes. Bekka found a nurse's uniform and two floor-length dresses. Her mother added a shawl for her arms if it got cold at night and a

bonnet in case the girls had to wear something on their heads. Girls dressed very differently back then. She and her friend Hannah practiced running and going upstairs with skirts that touched the ground. It was going to be harder than it looked not to trip and fall.

Ben and his friends thought they looked cool in the old-style dark blue army clothes made for young reenactors. Their hats had rifles that crossed each other—similar to those worn by soldiers.

A week before they left, Mr. Dupries got a picture of everyone in their clothes to put in the school yearbook. He had them run two laps around the gym to make sure everyone could run and move without ripping them. No one was allowed to wear modern clothing at Gettysburg or take electronic devices like video games or cellphones. Cameras were allowed since they had been invented at the time of the Civil War.

Ben's thoughts usually drifted toward food. He loved to eat and hoped the food would taste good. He heard they cooked meals in pots in holes in the ground. His grandmother's family cookbook said they could even make cherry pies in one. He hoped when it was his turn to make a meal, cherry pie was on the menu. *What if we burn our food?* Ben wondered. *No McDonald's or Burger King or Taco Bell to the rescue.* That was a scary thought.

Finally, the day to leave arrived. It took over an hour to stuff everyone's luggage and supplies into a trailer and then another ten minutes for mothers to quit hugging and kissing their kids

good-bye. You would think they were leaving for a month. Ben was glad his mom wasn't mushy like that. It would be so embarrassing.

The two-day bus trip from Lansing to Gettysburg was long, and at one point, it was bone-chilling. They crossed the state line from Michigan into Ohio and neared Lake Erie. It was the first time for many to see one of the five Great Lakes. Ben and Bekka had been to beaches at Lake Michigan and Lake Huron, but hadn't been in Ohio to see Lake Erie. The bus driver stopped at a park so the class could have their picture taken by the lakeshore. Brave ones, including Ben and Bekka, took off their shoes and socks to wade into it, but the lake was so cold from being frozen during the winter, they mainly got their big toes wet.

It didn't take long after that to see the sign stating, 'Welcome to Pennsylvania, the Keystone State.' Ben wondered what the Keystone was. He'd ask Bekka to look it up in her travel book which she took every time they went on trips. She was forever reading 'little known facts' and using them as an FYI—*For Your Information.* Like with the snakes. She hated snakes and studied pictures of them so she would know which ones were poisonous if they saw one. She even read about sucking out venom if someone got bit by one. He guessed nurses might not mind doing it. But not him! No way was he sucking venom out of anyone's leg or arm, even if it was his twin sister. Well, maybe, if it might save her life. But he didn't think very long about it since Mrs. Haynie, their school nurse, was with them. She could handle the gross stuff.

The best part of the trip was spending the night in a hotel. They stayed up past their normal bedtime watching "The Wizard

of Oz" and filling up on popcorn made fresh in the lobby. Ben ate until his stomach bulged—just in case they had to eat wild pig or turnip greens. He read someplace those were normal foods in the 1860s. Not for him! Bring on tacos, burgers, chips, dip, and chocolate chip cookies. Those were normal foods.

BOOM! Another blast brought Ben out of his thoughts and made him duck again in case a stray cannonball came his way.

Chapter 4

Smoke from the cannon rose forming a cloud over the tents. They'd never seen or heard anything like it before.

Bekka put her hands over her ears. "Those cannon blasts are so loud. Do you think they're doing target practice?"

Stephen pointed toward a man shoving a black handle into the opening of the cannon. "Looks like they're loading it again. What's going on?"

"I don't know, but let's put our bags in our tent and change into our army uniforms," Ben said, picking up his duffel bag. "I hope my pillow is still with my sleeping bag. Mr. Dupries said all we have in our tents are two cots, a table and two chairs."

"If it isn't there," Stephen informed him, "you can make a pillow with straw and wrap your shirt around it. My grandma said that's what the soldiers did, and then bugs got in them and bit them in the head when they were sleeping."

"Yuk!" Just thinking about it made Bekka start scratching her head—after she took off her bonnet. She and Hannah had wasted no time getting into their old-fashioned clothes. She kind of liked her outfit. It made her feel like one of the girls from "Little House on the Prairie."

"Hannah and I got our stuff unpacked fast," she stated. "My pillow is safe and sound away from all bed bugs. Hannah is wandering around taking pictures of everything. Her mother told her she could make a poster of our trip, so she doesn't want to miss a thing."

"Bekka!" her friend called behind her. Turning, a flash went off in front of her face.

"Aw, Hannah—I wasn't looking," Bekka moaned, as she squinted her eyes. Grabbing her bonnet and posing, she said, "Take one of me with my hat on. No, Ben, you take one of both of us in our dresses. We think we look cute."

Hannah gave her camera to Ben, and put her head next to Bekka's, all the while saying, "cheese-whiz." It was all Ben could do not to gag.

"Oh, brother, you girls think you have to have a picture of everything. Did anyone tell the kids from the South and all those ladies in their really big poofy skirts that Miss Shutterbug and her friend will be stalking them with a camera this week?"

Ben just didn't get it. Why take so many pictures?

Hannah took the camera and defended herself. "This is our hobby. Mr. Dupries said everyone should have a hobby, and we decided taking pictures is our hobby. And I have a message from Mr. Dupries. He said to put your stuff in the tent and be at the flagpole in ten minutes with your Gettysburg clothes on."

Ben and Stephen threw their duffel bags into what might be their unlucky tent. It was kind of big—big enough for all their stuff, and had a pole in the middle making it tall enough for adults. They had two cots, one on each side of the pole, plus two chairs next to a very small table.

They went in search of their sleeping bags, which were among others in a big pile at the drop-off point out near the road. It was amazing how much stuff was on their bus.

Ben spotted his sleeping bag and grabbed it. "Being here is so cool. This is the best field trip I've ever taken." He looked around at all the open fields surrounding them. There were cannons, monuments, and many information signs telling what

happened in fields like the Peach Orchard, Devil's Den, and Little Round Top. It was awesome to be in such a famous place. He was glad to have Stephen, a relative of famous General Farnsworth, as his friend and tent mate.

Stephen's duffel bag was farther down in the pile. "Who would have thought being a Farnsworth would make me famous? My grandma can't wait for me to tell her all about it." He tugged on the bag and threw it over to the side. "Now to find my secret weapon."

Stephen stepped over other people's luggage, looking for a long black canvas bag. He had been given special permission to bring something no one usually is allowed to use. He couldn't wait to show it to Ben.

"You brought a weapon?" Ben asked, rather shocked.

"Yep, there it is," he said, jogging over to get it. Ben had no idea what he was talking about.

Alone in their tent, Stephen pulled a long-handle tool out of the bag. Ben's eyebrows shot up half way to his hair.

"What is that?" Ben asked, shocked his friend hadn't told him about it before now.

"It's a metal detector." Stephen ran his hand down the handle. "My grandmother told me my great-great-great-grandfather lost his wedding ring when he was here, and she got permission for me to bring this and try to find it near Little Round Top battlefield where he fought. Usually they don't let anyone bring a metal detector

here to Gettysburg, but because this is a field trip for kids, and since I'm related to General Farnsworth, they said I could try to find his ring if it is still in these fields. Mrs. Ranes says I shouldn't get my hopes up, but you never know. I just might get lucky." He circled it over the grass pretending he was in search of buried treasure.

Ben reached for it. "Wow, I wonder what else we might find when you're using it. Let's try it now, here in our tent."

"Can't," Stephen said, pulling it back toward him. "Right now we have to be at the flagpole with our clothes on remember?"

Stephen didn't want to get into trouble with his metal detector on the first day. He hoped they would find something old and rare here in the park. Ben's dad would add that to the story he was writing about the school field trip for the Lansing newspaper. Being one of the State Journal's top reporters, Mr. Cooper was sure to mention Stephen's name if he made history for himself. Ben and Bekka seemed to be following in his footsteps because they were good at finding the who, what, when, where, why, and how of a story. Their dad said they had a "nose for the news," because they had a way of solving mysterious happenings. Just a couple of months ago, they discovered the crooks stealing band instruments from the school just before the Spring Concert. Mrs. Ranes was so thankful, she gave them each a twenty-five dollar savings bond and a Good Citizen Certificate. Stephen hoped he might get involved in a story which could make the headlines.

They put the metal detector under Stephen's cot and got into their clothes as fast as they could. Because zippers hadn't been invented by the 1860s, they had to button up their pants, which slowed them down. Their dark blue shirts had plenty of buttons too—quite a difference between that and pulling a t-shirt over their heads.

"Doing up all these buttons is crazy!" Ben said as he tucked in his shirt and pulled on his leather boots. "I hope I can run in these things." They weren't the same as sneakers.

Stephen stomped his feet in his leather boots. "Yeah, I ran around my yard at home to test my boots. They're kind of slippery

on the bottom. But it's kind of cool to see how kids lived back then. Come on, we gotta get going."

Before they left, they unrolled their sleeping bags on the cots and laid their pillows on top. For just a minute, Ben laid on his cot to test what it was going to feel like tonight when they went to bed. Not too bad, he thought, but not much room to roll over. The cot was half the size of his twin bed, so he wondered if he might find himself on the ground if he moved too much in his sleep.

They stuffed their regular clothes into their bags and threw them into a corner. The sun was beginning to warm their canvas tent, causing it be hot and stuffy, and giving off a strong smell that made them want to get out of there. Just then a whistle blew and the boys flew out of their tent. They raced to the flagpole along with more than one hundred other kids looking like they had just stepped out of a history book. A one-hundred-and-fifty-year-old history book.

Chapter 5

Bekka and Hannah held up their skirts as they ran across the field to the flagpole. Sure enough, Bekka almost tripped as she stepped into a rut in the ground.

"How did girls run back then?" she gasped, tugging on her dress which was under her shoe.

"I don't know, but we'll soon learn," Hannah replied, holding tightly to her camera so it wouldn't go flying should she trip, too.

"Listen up, everyone," a ranger called, as the students and teachers came from every direction. He was dressed in his National Park Ranger uniform and looked very official.

"Good morning. My name is Ranger Moore, and I want to welcome all of you to Gettysburg. Many of you have come a long way to be here. Some of you live in Pennsylvania, so it wasn't a long trip, but many of you traveled several hundred miles and we welcome you to our beautiful and historical state. That is why you all came, isn't it? To live out history? Actually, you're making history because this is the 150th year since the battle of Gettysburg, and you are participating in a reenactment where it all happened."

The adults thought it was cool and started clapping loudly. Before long, everyone else joined in. When they had quieted, the ranger continued.

"In a few minutes, I'll have you get into teams. Northern states will be on this side of the flagpole and Southern states on that side." He waved his arm on each side of the pole indicating where the teams should go.

On the North's side was a red, white, and blue Stars and Stripes flag. It had thirty-four stars representing the thirty-four states in the Union. On the Southern side was a Confederate Battle flag—red, white, and blue with thirteen stars.

"I see the North's army has on blue clothing, while the South's army is in gray—just like it was back then."

Everyone looked around to see that the boys were a mixture of nationalities, all about the same height, dressed in blue and gray clothes. The adult men teachers matched the clothing of their students. Ladies and girls were allowed to wear any color they wanted since they didn't fight in the war. There were nurses and aides, but they didn't have matching uniforms.

"I hope you're looking forward to our special reenactment," the ranger continued. "We think it'll be one you'll remember the rest of your lives. I see some of you brought cameras. Take as many pictures as you can because your families will want to see what happened here."

Hannah smiled and held up her camera. She took a lot of teasing because she was forever taking pictures—but she was the one who had proof of how goofy her friends acted when they got together. She blinked her eyes and made herself focus on the ranger's instructions, not last weekend's sleepover and the boatload of pictures she and Bekka took.

"I want to tell you a few things about our park. The official name is Gettysburg National Military Park. It isn't like a city park with swings and a ball diamond. This is a place dedicated to the memory of those who fought here during the Civil War on the first three days of July in 1863. A national park is protected by men and women called rangers. We have responsibilities, like giving tours around the battlefields and answering any questions, as well

as keeping a watchful eye on all activity. A national park is different in another way. Can anyone tell me what that is?"

No one answered until Mrs. Ranes spoke up. "You may not damage the park in any way or take anything out of it."

"Correct. This park is very special and has many memories connected with it. If you should find an old object lying around, please give it to a teacher or one of us rangers. We have shelves in our museums filled with guns, bullets, metal buttons, silverware, parts of rifles—all things which have been found since the 1860s. Who knows; maybe there is something more for us to add to the collection." Stephen and Ben looked at each other and smiled. Using the metal detector just might prove to be very useful for the park's museum, too.

"Should you see something suspicious happening, or notice something is missing, please tell an adult in your group or come to me. You are our eyes and ears to help protect our park and make sure it is the same when you leave as it was when you arrived." Ranger Moore didn't want them to think there were dishonest people in the group, but no one knew everybody or what they were thinking. It was just a warning he gave to every group that came for events. Sometimes it paid off and bad plots were foiled.

"One last thing before you get into your teams. I want to tell you about a special program national parks have. It's called the Junior Ranger program." He held up a booklet about the size of a magazine. "National parks want young people your age to enjoy the time they spend in the parks. We have booklets, available at

the Visitor Center, for you to work on as you go from site to site. You'll learn the history of the battlefields and discover things for yourself. There are questions to answer and assignments to work on. When your book is filled in, take it to the information desk in the Visitor Center, and a ranger will stamp it. We also have Gettysburg patches you can buy. You might want to start a collection of patches for yourself as you travel to other national parks across the country. Most parks have this program, and it's a great way to learn about the parks while you are there."

Teachers were nodding that they thought it was a great idea. Bekka thought so. She would work hard to finish her book and have a picture taken with the ranger. She was collecting things for her bedroom to make a Wall of Fame—a picture of her with a real Gettysburg Ranger would be impressive.

"Alright, now let's get into our forma..." Just then, another blast went off, and Ranger Moore ducked in surprise. All heads turned toward a hill in the distance.

Chapter 6

"How could I forget about the cannon blasts?"

Ranger Moore wasn't prepared for the blast and practically jumped out of his skin, sending his hat flying to the ground. He bent over, picked it up, and kept talking. "You'll be hearing plenty of cannons going off this week. During the three days of battle here at Gettysburg, the noise of hundreds of cannons never quit. We want you to experience some of what the soldiers experienced. One big difference, though," he said with a twinkle in his eyes, "our cannonballs won't be shot in a direction where there are people." He gave the kids time to laugh over that one. "Now, please get with your teams and let's see what the North and South looks like today."

Sixty-three fifth graders from the South faced sixty-six fifth graders from the North in their blue and gray clothing and long dresses. Teachers had on similar clothes, only in larger sizes. Mr. Dupries wore suspenders, making him look kind of like a grandpa. Ben, Stephen, and their friend, Ethan, snickered when they saw him. Hannah just had to get a picture him. It could go in the yearbook under Most Memorable Moment.

The ranger quieted everyone down and began talking again. "You're probably wondering what we're going to do each day. When the armies moved from place to place, in addition to their weapons, they took their tents, cots, food, and cooking wagons.

Speaking of cooking, you'll each have a turn making a meal—1860s style. As you can see, we don't have stoves out here in the fields, so we'll eat and cook like they did."

Everyone turned their heads to see where the cooking places might be and wondered what they would be eating for the next nine meals. They weren't allowed to bring snacks, and the thought of eating weird food was frightening to some of them. Being a picky eater could lead to starvation.

Ranger Moore startled them with his next statement. "Back in the 1860s, they used the ground as a cooking area. They dug holes and built fires in them which lasted until the food was done cooking. I think you'll be surprised how good the food tastes. In fact, our head cook, Mrs. Hopewell, has a recipe which her own children like to eat. We'll have copies of it for you to take home and cook with your families when you go camping. Most importantly, please, don't burn our food. It's all we have—and we still have to eat it."

Many boys dropped their jaws because they loved to eat, and having burned food served didn't appeal to them. Some held their stomachs and made faces. Ethan was one of them. He lived to eat. Food was the first thing on his mind every morning. He woke up hungry—he just couldn't help it.

"One last thing before the fun begins—I ask that you respect the personal property of each person here and don't touch or take something that doesn't belong to you. We're here for a good time and if each of us lives by the Golden Rule of treating others as we

would want to be treated, we won't have any problems. No one goes into anyone else's tent without permission. Got that?"

Responses of "yes" and "yes, sir" were heard from each side of the flagpole.

"Only adults, like a teacher, a nurse, the laundry lady, or a ranger can enter a student's tent when they aren't present. Got that?"

Louder "yes" and "yes, sir" rose from the students.

"Good. Now, let's get on with our version of the Battle at Gettysburg. Rather than using guns and rifles, you'll be using shuttlecocks, sticks, hoops, and cat's eyes."

"What?" Looks of confusion shown on many faces.

"Yes, boys and girls, to give you a feeling of what it was like for children back in the 1860s, your reenactment on these battlefields will be 'The Games of Gettysburg.' Those of you from the North will compete against those of you from the South, playing games known to children back then. You'll wear your clothing and shoes, and use only the game equipment they had. Things were different. In the case of balls, they didn't have rubber balls, baseballs, or anything made of plastic. They had wooden balls or leather ones stuffed with beans or cotton. Each day we'll give you instructions for the game and we'll keep track of who wins and who loses. For each winning school from the North and the South, we have a trophy in the shape of a monument to take back for your

classroom. They're a one-of-a-kind trophy, so you'll definitely want to help your side win. Are you excited?"

A roar of "yeah" and "yes, sir" went up from the crowd.

"Who's going to win?"

"The South!"

"The North!"

Everyone jumped up and down, giving high-fives to strangers, acting like they were sure to win the trophies, and bragging rights.

Chapter 7

"Before you start playing, you need to get to know your teammates better. Those of you from Michigan, New York, and Pennsylvania, go get your blue name tags over at that table." Ranger Moore pointed to a table where Mrs. Ranes and Miss Iversen had markers and stacks of name tags.

"All of you from South Carolina, Virginia, and Georgia, go to that table and get your gray name tags." Two teachers stood ready with markers and name tags for their students.

It didn't take long before kids were talking to each other. Ben and Bekka met Sean, Luke, and Morgan from Pennsylvania, while Stephen and Hannah met Danielle, Zoe, and David from New York.

On the other side of the flagpole, Ashley from Virginia met Rachel and Evan from Georgia, while Kaitlyn from South Carolina met C.P. and Taylor from Virginia. Some were excited to meet new people while others seemed a bit quiet and shy.

The name tags saved the day! After meeting twenty new people, remembering who was who was completely impossible! Bekka remembered names easily, but Ben couldn't. He needed to hear a person's name at least twice, and then it was in his memory. But until then, it saved a lifetime of embarrassment by looking at a name tag. He wasn't alone, everyone was doing it.

Students told each other what sports they played at school but none used a shuttlecock, hoop, stick, and definitely not cats' eyes. That was disgusting, just disgusting.

Ranger Moore blew his whistle signaling for them to listen again. Ben's stomach was rumbling. He hoped the subject of food would soon come up. It had been quite awhile since he ate his two bowls of cereal at the hotel. Much to his relief, food was the new subject.

"Today's lunch is an easy one. Our cooks roasted chickens this morning for you to make a chicken sandwich on homemade bread. You can take a pickle from the large wooden barrel and a bright red apple, which was grown over there in the orchard. Remember, all foods back then were made from scratch, so this is the beginning of your 1863 adventure. After you eat, meet me at the Visitor Center where you'll get your Junior Ranger booklet and then get started with the first game."

The huge trays of chicken were amazing—no one had ever seen that much meat before in all of their lives. They were amazed to see pickles stored in a large wooden barrel and wondered how come the juice didn't run out. Bekka and Hannah's faces shriveled up like prunes when they bit into the sourest, dilliest big ole dill pickle ever! Ben needed a camera but neither gave him theirs. Their faces should have been on Hannah's poster!

Ranger Moore had stacks of Junior Ranger books ready to give each student after lunch. They immediately opened them to see what the assignments were like. He led them to a theater

where they watched a video on the Battle at Gettysburg. Some understood for the first time the great division in our country and why the battle happened. They saw pictures of the army of the South wearing gray, and the army of the North wearing blue. All of them recognized President Lincoln, but didn't know he had taken a train to Gettysburg four months after the battle, or that he knew the Morse code using dots and dashes to send telegraph messages to generals during the Civil War. Ben's Uncle Chris used Morse code to send messages around the world. Maybe he would learn it. How difficult could it be?

Lost in his thoughts, Ben didn't hear the instructions being given, so he just followed everyone back outdoors to the flagpole. Ranger Moore explained everyone would get a bag of supplies needed for all of the games. They were responsible to keep them in their tents and not lose anything. Otherwise they would forfeit their opportunity to play that game. Several rangers handed bags to the students. No one could resist looking at the contents, seeing things for the first time ever.

"All of you have a feather object, called a shuttlecock, in your bag. You'll need it for the first game. When I blow my whistle, I want you to go back to your tents, leave your Junior Ranger books and your bag of game supplies, and come back with only your shuttlecock. Go!"

Chapter 8

Everyone scattered to their tents, returning in less than five minutes. Excitement was rising on both sides of the flagpole. Mrs. Ranes, Miss Iversen, and most of the ladies had trouble walking quickly in their big hooped skirts. It was hard keeping up with students. Bekka wondered if the women wished they could wear pants like the men.

Once everyone returned, Ranger Moore explained that Shuttlecock was like Badminton, played with small rackets and a ball with feathers attached. That was called the shuttlecock.

They would be playing at the volleyball nets which were in the field near the Visitor's Center. Two students from each state were assigned to play against two students from the opposing side. They had to hit the shuttlecock over the net and keep hitting it until someone missed and it hit the ground. When someone missed, the other team scored a point. The first team to reach fifteen points would win the match. Teachers would keep score.

It looked kind of easy, but keeping the shuttlecock in the air proved to be a challenge. Ben and Ethan were opposite Rachel and Evan from Georgia. Ben was sure he could hit it to Rachel and she'd miss hitting it back, so he hit it as hard as he could, sending it flying over the net. Even though she was in a long skirt, Rachel ran under the shuttlecock and hit it back. Ethan dove for it and missed, hitting his racket on the ground as he fell.

"Ow," he groaned as he spit out grass. "Guess I won't try that again."

Rachel grinned. Sometimes it felt good to show boys how well girls could play games.

"Girls," he muttered to Ben while shaking his head. "You just can't be sure how good they're going to be."

"Yeah, sometimes they surprise you."

They volleyed the shuttlecock back and forth five times before Evan swung and missed. It was their longest volley and they all felt like champs. The two boys won the point. It was going to be a long game.

Bekka didn't let her long skirt stop her from going after the shuttlecock either. With a racket in her right hand and skirt lifted up by her left hand, she flew toward the net determined to hit it back over. With a stretch of her arm, she gave it a good whack. Being athletic helped. She liked to win, so tried to be good at all sports. She thought it might be fun to have a game of badminton at home. She and Ben might just show their parents how good they were.

At three o'clock, the cannon went off signaling the end of the game. Teachers reported scores and added them together while the students hiked to another area for the next game. Wooden circles, resembling small hula hoops and sticks lay in straight lines across the field.

"It looks like some of you were getting pretty good at shuttlecock," Ranger Moore stated. "Who do you think won?"

"The North!"

"The South!"

"That's what I thought you'd say."

Everyone groaned. They wanted to know, right then.

"We'll reveal the scores at the end of the day, so keep playing at your highest level. And keep being good sports. For those who like to run, we have a game called Hoops and Sticks. This one is not so easy either. It will be a relay race-North against the South. Half of each school will be at the other end of the field. You have to roll your hoop down the field to the person waiting at the line,

pushing it only with your stick, When you are finished, play it again. Your teachers will observe who wins each round. On your mark, get set, go!"

Skateboarding down a mud mountain would have been easier than chasing a hoop with a stick across the field. Ben's hoop got caught in the wind and sailed down a hill out of control. It was incredibly hard rolling it back uphill using only his stick. He couldn't be sure if his team was ahead or behind because there were kids running in every direction trying to get their hoops across the finish line.

When the cannon went off, sweat poured off everyone from the hot sun and running to fetch runaway hoops.

"Water, I need water," Stephen called out, collapsing on the ground. He wasn't alone in wanting a drink.

"It looks like a water break is in order," Ranger Moore announced. "No water bottles here. We'll do it the old-fashioned way." Much to their amazement, rangers handed out metal cups which the boys and girls dipped into a huge bucket of water.

"No double dipping!" the ranger called out. "Get a clean cup here."

"Am I dreaming, or am I really at the "Little House on the Prairie?" Bekka asked as she dipped and then sipped her drink.

"I don't know and I don't care," Ben stated. "I just need to get more water." His throat was so dry; he needed his own bucket to get enough.

Chapter 9

Everyone had free time to relax while New York and South Carolina made dinner. Most went to their tents to talk with friends and try out their cots. Earlier, while they were busy playing games, a staff member put a lantern, a pitcher of water, and two washcloths on the table in each tent. Ben and Stephen couldn't wait until it got dark to light their lantern.

Soon the smell of dinner cooking drifted toward the tents. Whatever was cooking smelled delicious, making everyone realize how hungry they were getting. At five o'clock, the dinner bell rang.

"Beans were plentiful during the war so were served every day," Mrs. Hopewell, the head cook, explained when they were all gathered at the tables. "Our dinner this evening will be bean soup and more of our homemade bread."

Just the mention of bean soup made many wrinkle up their noses, but knowing there wasn't anything else to eat, everyone took a bowlful and ate it. To their surprise, it tasted better than they thought it would. Dessert was served in washtubs—slices of cool, sweet watermelon—now that hit the spot.

Just for the fun of it, C.P. from Virginia challenged someone from the North to a watermelon seed-spitting contest.

"I bet I can spit a watermelon seed farther than any of all y'all!" he boasted.

"Maybe you can, maybe you can't," Sean from Pennsylvania called back. His family often had watermelon at picnics so he and Luke had seed-spitting contests all the time. He felt he stood a good chance against C.P., so to prove it, Sean rolled his tongue around a seed to get it really wet, and let it fly. It was a challenge C.P. couldn't refuse.

Mr. Dupries had both boys come to the front of the eating area with several seeds in their hands. "You each get three chances to spit a seed. Select three of your friends to stand by a seed after you spit it and we'll see who the champ really is."

Both boys selected friends who they could trust and went to stand by Mr. Dupries. Sean and C.P. each put a seed in his mouth. Cheering sections formed and got loud. Mr. Dupries had to speak louder than the crowd.

"C.P., since you voiced the challenged, you can go first."

When he was good and ready, C.P. let his first seed fly out of his mouth. Kids who stood nearby jumped back, being sure spit would come out with the seed. All eyes watched it sail through the air. His friend ran to stand at the spot where the seed fell.

"Sean, let's see if you can match it."

Sean rolled the seed around in his mouth and flung it as far as he could. After it landed, his friend was right on the spot. It landed three inches short of where C.P.'s seed lay. There were boos for him and cheers for C.P., who fist-pumped the air and yelled, "Yeah!" Excitement rose.

Sean started the second round with another seed going an inch beyond C.P's first seed. That was more like it—he knew he could do it! Now the cheers were for him. That got both boys pumped up.

Much to his dismay, C.P.'s second seed just couldn't match it, falling short of Sean's distance mark. He was losing his touch. He shook his head in disgust and kicked at the grass.

"This is it, boys," Mr. Dupries stated, looking left and right at the two boys. "These are your last seeds. Will the challenger stand or fall?"

At that point, every observer got quiet and stared at Sean, who let his third seed fly. It went higher than it did far, so landed way shorter than his other two. But his first one was still out front by an inch. Pressure was now on C.P. to prove his claim that he was the King-of-the-Hill watermelon seed-spitter. Sean was quite confident C.P. couldn't do it.

C.P. put the last seed in his mouth and rolled it around on his tongue. He inhaled through his nose and put the most force ever into making it sail through the air as he let it fly! Spit even came out with it. No one cared. Mr. Dupries didn't take his eyes off the seed, knowing it was going to be close. It looked to be floating in the air in slow motion, landing just a half inch beyond Sean's, proving C.P. was the best of the best watermelon seed-spitters! The noise was deafening. The Southern boy won! Uncontrolled excitement was in the air for C.P.'s victory. They were so pumped up, they bragged they'd win every single game and competition. They were on a roll thanks to the boy from Virginia. They would soon see.

BOOM! The cannon went off again signaling the start of the last game of the day. Ranger Moore held up his hand to speak.

"This morning I mentioned that you would be playing with cats' eyes."

"Cats' eyes. Ew-w-w." Several girls squealed and shuddered.

"Co-ol," a boy called out over the girls' voices.

"It's not what you think. Each of you was given a big bag with your game supplies." He held up a small cloth bag. "It contains a small bag that looks like this. In it are your cats' eyes. Run back to your tents and get them. Five extra points to the side that gets back here first. Go!"

Chapter 10

Everyone dashed to their tents and opened their bags to see if there were petrified cats' eyes in them. Seeing none, they grabbed their little cloth bags and dashed back to be first to the flagpole. Straight lines angled out from the flagpole and teachers counted as students returned.

"Five points to the Northern team—you won by two shakes of a lamb's tail." High fives, cheering, and clapping went on until Ranger Moore whistled and held up his bag. After losing to C.P. earlier, this evened the score.

"The game of Marbles has been around for hundreds, maybe thousands of years. They have been made of clay, metal and glass. Most likely, many soldiers had marbles in their pockets and fingered them as they walked from town to town with their army units. Open your bag and look inside. You'll see a lot of small marbles and one large one. They have many colors and designs. Those that are clear with a swirl in the center are called cats' eyes. Some of you girls look relieved that you aren't going to play with the real thing." A ripple of giggles came from some of them.

"Over the years, the rules for the game of marbles have changed, and it has been played many ways. If you were able to ask your great-grandfathers how they played down South, it would be different than how it was played up North, and from state to state. However, we will have only one set of rules.

“A person from the North will play a person from the South. Since they didn’t have paved parking lots in the 1860s, we will go to the dirt path over there. Each team of two people will draw a circle in the dirt about two feet across. Both players will drop five marbles in the circle. Since C.P. won the watermelon seed-spitting contest, the person from the South goes first.”

Cheers went up for C.P.’s seed-spitting ability. He waved his arms above his head, like he was the heavy-weight champion of the world.

“Go, C.P.! Go, C.P.!” A group of girls had quickly formed a cheerleading squad. Ranger Moore quieted them down.

“Back to the instructions. Your big marble is called an ally. That will be your shooter. You will place it anywhere on the outside of the circle and aim to hit one of the marbles in the circle to knock it out of the circle. To properly shoot your ally marble, your hand has to be resting on the ground. Bend your first finger forward and with your knuckle touching the ground, push your thumbnail into your finger. This is called knuckling-down. Place your large marble in front of your thumb nail and flick it as hard as you can. If your marble hits your opponent’s marble and it goes out of the circle, you get to keep it. It is still your turn until you don’t hit one out. Then it is the other person’s turn. When the cannon sounds, show your teacher how many marbles you have in your possession. Then meet me back here. Okay, get your assigned opponent and may the best team win!”

Rangers drew sixty-two circles in the dirt path while the students met their challengers. This was a new game to everyone. Most had a bunch of marbles at home from old games, but no one knew there was a real game which had been played since before America was discovered.

Boys stared into the eyes of the guys opposite them—beginning a mental challenge. The clank of marbles hitting each other began to fill the air. Groans were heard as allies missed the intended marble. Others let out whoops and hollers and pumped the air with their fists when they saw marble after marble roll out of the circle.

Bekka, playing against Taylor from Virginia, met her match when it came to winning. Both girls bent low to the ground to make sure their shooter marble was lined up exactly to hit the target hard enough.

"Have you ever done this before?" Hannah asked. "You play like an expert."

"No, but I don't like to lose. I learn how to play and try hard to win."

"Me too. I have a twin brother, Ben, whom I like to play against and beat."

"You have a twin brother? That must be fun. I wish I had a brother or a sister. It would be fun to have someone my own age to play with. I'm an only child. My dad plays with me. He says it's

not good if he lets me win all the time, and makes me try to beat him. He says it's a good challenge."

Bekka couldn't imagine living without her brother. She felt sorry for Taylor, so asked, "Want to be friends? I never had a friend from Virginia before. We can write to each other and maybe someday my family can come see your family. My stepsister lives at a camp in North Carolina. Do you live near North Carolina?"

"I'm not sure. I'll have to ask my teacher. And yeah, let's be friends. I'd like that."

As they talked, they kept playing, trying to end up with the most marbles. They were down to just one marble left in the circle. Taylor took her best shot and missed. Bekka felt sorry she might beat Taylor, but couldn't pass up the win. She really did want to see a trophy in her classroom, so she put her shooter by her thumbnail and flicked it as hard as she could. The noise of the two

marbles clanking together was music to her ears, and watching them roll across the line was like icing on a cake. She won the match and threw her arms up in the air. She couldn't help but squeal. Both girls talked about how they were going to take their marbles home and play against their grandparents. They were pretty sure they could beat them!

Five minutes later—**BOOM!** The cannons went off sending smoke into the air once again. Winners eagerly ran to the teachers to report how many marbles they had in their possession.

The teachers were kept busy keeping accurate scores of wins and losses. None wanted their team to lose. Each had an idea of where they could put the trophy in their classrooms. Mr. Dupries planned to have a very large picture made of his winning team and their trophy hung in the hallway. To him, these games were as big as the Olympics.

"May I have your attention, please?" yelled Ranger Moore into his bullhorn.

Chapter 11

"Teachers, please report your scores to me as soon as possible so we can announce today's winner. Students, you may go to your tents for free time until we have something to report."

"Yahoo!" yelled Ben as he and Stephen ran across the field to their tent. Time to test the metal detector. Stephen had promised Ben he could be the first one to test it, so he could hardly wait.

"I think I'll bury some of my jacks in the grass and you can find them," Stephen offered. "They're metal, so it should start buzzing as soon as you get near one."

"Sweet!" Ben couldn't wait to see how sensitive it was.

As Ben pulled the metal detector from under Stephen's cot and removed it from the bag, Stephen took his bag of jacks and went outside. He used his jackknife to dig small holes to push six jacks down into the ground. He stepped back toward the tent and told Ben to turn the detector on.

Ben started moving it over the grass in a circular pattern. Almost immediately, the detector started clicking like crazy. As he got over a spot, the clicks sped up. Ben let out a howl and turned it off. He bent down and soon found the hole Stephen had made. The noise of the metal detector and Ben's hollering drew a lot of

attention. Before long, he had a crowd hovering nearby, watching what was going on.

Most had never seen a metal detector and thought it was really cool. Many wanted to try it too, so got their jacks from their tents, and had their friends dig holes and hide them. It was like they were digging for gold. Just about everyone got a turn to use it.

Someone asked Stephen why he brought it, so he held up his fingers and counted as he told the story of his great-great-great-great-great-great-great-grandfather who had fought on those battlefields and lost his wedding ring, and that he had gotten special permission to bring a metal detector, just this once, to search for the ring. It made him feel like a hero to be doing something so special for his family. It made everyone want to help him look for it too.

"Ben's dad is a reporter and said he would write a story if I found it," Stephen also informed them. "Just think—finding a ring buried for a hundred and fifty years. My grandma would go crazy! Who knows, we just might find other stuff buried here that no one knows about under this grass. We might all become famous!"

Mr. Dupries saw the crowd of kids and came wandering over. He spotted the metal detector and asked Stephen if he had been looking for his great grandpa's ring yet.

"No, we just were hiding jacks in the grass and finding them. It's really sensitive and goes off even when something is a short distance away. Watch."

Stephen turned it on and moved it toward Mr. Dupries' shoe which had a metal buckle on top of it. The clicking noise started almost immediately, surprising his teacher.

"Wow! No wonder people take them to beaches and fields looking for money or other valuables. I've heard they lead to great finds and people get rewards from owners. It makes you wonder if you might find more than your grandpa's ring. Just remember to turn over anything you find to Ranger Moore, including the ring. They keep records of everything they find. Maybe tomorrow during our free time, our class can walk around this whole area and over there near the trees with the detector. I'd love to see your grandmother's face if you bring home your great-great-grandpa's ring."

"Can we do that?" Stephen asked, surprised his teacher was willing to let him use the metal detector so long.

"Ranger Moore and his staff know you brought it and I'll tell them you know to turn in anything you find. It makes you wonder what the most unusual item was ever found here. We'll have to ask at the information desk. Oh yes, speaking of the information desk, the Ranger at the Visitor's Center was wondering if any of you have worked on your Junior Ranger books. I told him 'no,' but we're planning on seeing the Cyclorama."

Ben's eyebrows went halfway up his forehead. "Cyclo-what?"

"The Cyclorama is a huge painting which shows the story of the three-day battle, the fields they fought in, which army was making advances on the other, and much, much more.

Ranger Moore thought it would be meaningful for everyone to see it. Plus, it is a Junior Ranger assignment. I believe it is the first thing we are doing tomorrow morning before we play the Games of Gettysburg, Day 2. "

"Sweet," Stephen said. "My grandpa was an artist, but he wasn't famous. He just painted horses and dogs and things for the fun of it."

"I'm not good at art," his teacher admitted. "My family makes fun of me because the best I can do is stick figures. In fact, I would be a very good artist for any books with stick figures. I could become famous."

"It's okay, Mr. Dupries. We think you're the best teacher ever. Like my grandpa says, "no one is good at everything, just good at some things."

"Are you trying to butter me up, Ben, so I'll give you a good grade in Spelling?"

"Spelling... Ugh. I hate spelling. Bekka is the good speller. Mr. Dupries, do you know how to spell "dysentery"? She read in one of her travel books that you shouldn't drink water in certain places or you'll get sick, and now she thinks she's the Queen Bee of Spelling 'cause she knows how to spell dys-en-ter-y." He emphasized each syllable and shook his head from side to side. Ben wished just once Mr. Dupries would give him an A in spelling just for trying. A for affort, right?

BOOM! Everyone again jumped as the last cannon blast for the day sounded. There was no getting used to it. Over at the flagpole, Ranger Moore held up a trophy while another ranger beat on an old Civil War drum from the museum. Everyone came a runnin'. It looked like he had a big announcement.

Chapter 12

"This has been an outstanding day of competition between you youngsters from the North and South. You have shown great sportsmanship as you played shuttlecock, hoops and sticks, and with your cats' eyes. Your great-grandparents would have been proud, but also would have had a good laugh seeing you chase runaway hoops and diving into the ground for your shuttlecocks." There had been a lot of that and kids started laughing.

"Before I announce the winning side, I want you to show some appreciation to your teachers who worked hard to keep scores of who won and who came in second, if you know what I mean. Let's give them a round of applause." Kids clapped and some high-fived their teachers. It was a big job keeping the point totals accurate! Ranger Moore held up the clipboard to announce the day's winning side.

"Now for the moment you've all been waiting for. Teams from the South were better at hitting the shuttlecocks."

A big roar came up from the Southern teams. Ranger Moore held up his hand. "I wasn't finished. You Southerners know how to hit the shuttlecock well, but the teams from the North must have had better control over the hoops because they finished the relays first."

Now the Northerners burst out cheering. Everyone quieted down to hear the final score.

"Marbles proved to have the closest scores. Who do you think won?"

"The North!"

"The South!"

There was so much noise, Ranger Moore had to wait until everyone quieted down.

"Well, half of you are right!" Everyone held their breath as he held up the trophy again. "This is a traveling trophy. It will sit on a table next to the winning flag until I announce the winning team tomorrow night. And now, the team who shot their marbles best was… the SOUTH!"

Girls jumped up and down, squealing. Boys thumped each other on the back. Teachers even hugged students. Everyone was over-the-moon with excitement.

Except those from the North. They were stunned. Mr. Dupries tried to make his students feel better by telling them tomorrow was a new day and maybe they'd be the winner after other games were played. He believed in being good sports, so told his class to form a line and go over to the other side to congratulate the South.

It wasn't so bad smacking hands in a line. Some had become friends playing against each other so they felt like congratulating their new friends.

Ranger Moore was impressed with their good sportsmanship. "It's been a great day for all of us. Tomorrow morning we'll start off

by going to the Cyclorama where you'll see a famous painting of the three-day battle which took place in the fields surrounding us. Then we'll continue playing the Games of Gettysburg. Before bed tonight, you'll get a lesson from your teacher on the safety of using a lantern. Please use caution—you don't want to set anything on fire. And one last thing; tomorrow's meals will be brought to you by Michigan and Georgia.

"Michigan and Georgia," Ben repeated. Oh boy, I wonder what we have to cook. All of a sudden he remembered hearing that people ate pickled pig's feet back then. They wouldn't... they couldn't make us eat them, could they? NOOOO!

Chapter 13

Ben and Ethan walked back to the tents. When they got there, Stephen was dumping his bag of game supplies upside down on his sleeping bag. Ben looked at him like he was crazy.

"What are you doing?"

"My jacks are missing. They were here when I came for my bag of marbles and now they're gone. Did you do anything with my bag when you got your marbles?"

"No, I didn't touch your bag," Ben said emphatically.

"Well, somebody did!"

"Wasn't me. Someone must have come in here when we were playing marbles."

"That means I can't play tomorrow and it's an automatic loss for our team. We found all of them in the grass when we were using my metal detector, right?"

"Yeah, and we put them on the table after we put them back in the bag."

"Let's look under our beds and all around our tent before we tell anybody, just in case we didn't put them back in the bag." Stephen was already bending over just to make sure.

"But I know I put them back in your bag and put them on the table when you were putting your metal detector back under your cot." Ben knew what he was talking about.

"This isn't fair. I'm going to go tell Mr. Dupries," Stephen said, opening the flap of the tent to walk out.

"Wait. I'll go with you."

Both boys eyed everybody in sight—suspicious of strangers. *Who would have done this to Stephen? He's such a nice guy,* Ben thought as he walked toward their teacher.

Mr. Dupries and Ranger Moore listened to Stephen's story, not sure how to deal with it. Both felt sorry for him, but there were

no replacement jacks. If Stephen's jacks did not show up by the time of the games, he would have to forfeit.

Ranger Moore decided if there was something suspicious happening in the camp, he'd keep a closer eye on things. He knew there was the possibility that someone would take another person's games just to help their team win, but no one had reported seeing anyone going into someone else's tent. He had no one to suspect.

Stephen moped as he and Ben went back to their tent. Bekka and Hannah saw them coming and walked over to them.

"Where have you guys been?" Bekka asked, then noticed their faces. "What's wrong?"

"Somebody stole Stephen's jacks while we were playing marbles." Ben was looking around for anyone who might be watching them. He kept his voice a bit low.

"What? Somebody stole Stephen's jacks?"

"Sh! Keep your voice down," her brother said, giving her the evil eye. "We don't want everybody to hear, and if the guilty party is listening, we don't want him or her to know we know."

"What happened?" she asked, her voice was just above a whisper. They were back at the tent, so the four of them went inside to talk privately.

"We don't know. All we know is that someone came in and took Stephen's jacks and now he can't play tomorrow. He has to

forfeit his game. It's not fair. Who would do this? Maybe somebody is jealous because he has a metal detector."

"Did they take his metal detector, too?" Hannah asked.

"No, it's still under his cot, out of sight in the black bag."

Stephen kept looking around and under everything while the others talked. He even lifted his pillow and sleeping bag in case some mischievous person played a prank on him. Not a single jack was to be found.

"I told you this was an unlucky tent, Ben. It's only day one and already unlucky things are happening to me."

Ben looked at Bekka who looked at Hannah whose eyes were about to bug out of her head. Were Ben and Stephen in an unlucky tent? The girls didn't want to be there any longer. The sun was about to set and pretty soon it would be dark. They wanted to stay a safe distance away if the two boys were going to experience anything that might make them think it was... Just then their thoughts were interrupted by a loud voice outside.

"Everyone, please get your lanterns and come stand by your teacher," Ranger Moore said into a bullhorn.

Everyone from Michigan crowded around Mr. Dupries just as students from the other states surrounded their teachers. It was time to learn how to light a lantern safely. As Mr. Dupries gave detailed instructions on lighting the wick, the eyes and thoughts of the four young people roamed over to other groups. Who would want to sabotage Stephen's chances of winning, or the North's

chances of winning the jacks tournament and the trophy? It just didn't make any sense, since it was only one person's jacks that were missing.

They lit their lanterns and the four of them walked back to the boys' tent to talk until they had to go to bed. The glow sent shadows up to the ceiling causing their imaginations to go wild. They started making bunny ears on the wall with their hands in front of the light and soon they were making all kinds of shapes with their hands and arms and heads, making up goofy stories, and laughing their heads off.

Even Stephen got into it and forgot his fears of being in an unlucky tent or the victim of a plot. But he still wasn't sure if he wanted to turn out the lantern when Mr. Dupries came around at 10 o'clock, telling everyone it was time for lights out. Who knew what was lurking out there in the dark?

Bekka quickly journaled the day's events while Hannah put new batteries in her camera. She would be ready to snap a picture if something mysterious happened in the night. Her camera just might prove to be useful in more ways than one.

Chapter 14

"What is that?" Ben mumbled, as a horn blasted in the morning air. Not ready to get up, he pulled his pillow over his head. Sleeping on a narrow cot proved to be a bit more difficult than he imagined, and twice he found himself on the ground after rolling over the edge.

"It's a bugler playing revelry or something like that," Stephen informed him. "It's what they played to wake up soldiers." It was something his father said might happen.

"Is there a snooze button on that guy? Just give me ten more minutes, please." The bugler kept playing his wake up tune. No one could sleep through it, for sure.

Five cooks from Michigan and Georgia had volunteered to make breakfast of oatmeal and muffins. Ben and Bekka and their friends offered to do something more challenging. Ben talked to Mrs. Hopewell about making dinner in a cooking pot in the ground. He proclaimed himself "The Cast Iron Chef" by putting a pot on his head. Mrs. Hopewell removed it from his head and good-naturedly threatened to crown him if he didn't leave her cooking utensils where they belonged. Ben could be the class clown and make everyone laugh, which he often did.

"Just show up at three o'clock this afternoon and I'll show you how to make Mulligan stew and one of President Lincoln's favorite desserts—apple pie."

“Apple pie, my favorite,” Ben said, holding his stomach and rolling his eyes.

“Bet you never saw a meal cooked in a trench in the ground before,” Mrs. Hopewell said, washing off the cooking surface. “You’ll be amazed at how it’s done. Have fun with today’s games, just don’t break a leg. See you at three.”

They were off to join the rest of their classmates, who had their Junior Ranger books in hand, to visit the Cyclorama.

“We wondered where you guys were,” Mr. Dupries said, as they approached the tents. “Grab your books and let’s go. This is one history lesson you won’t forget for a long time.”

Everyone marched in single file to the Visitor’s Center where they listened and then studied a most amazing three-day battle painted on the wall. Having seen signs at several of the fields like the Wheatfield, Seminary Ridge, and Culp’s Hill, the students knew where the battles were fought. Wanting to go home with a Gettysburg patch, each one wrote answers to the questions in their Junior Ranger books. Stephen located Little Round Top on the map where his great...grandfather had fought. Bekka and Hannah took pictures to show their parents since none of them had ever been to Gettysburg.

“Bekka, come here,” her brother whispered, not wanting to disturb everyone, but wanting his sister to see the next adventure their group was going to have. “Look what they’re setting up in the field.”

“Cool,” she said, standing on tiptoes to look out a window. “I’ve always wanted to try that.” A huge smile came over here face as she mentally thought through the next competition. She was pretty sure she and Ben would be good at it even against a tough opponent.

Chapter 15

"What you are about to attempt is something else which children have played with for hundreds of years," Ranger Moore said fifteen minutes later while standing between a pair of stilts. He attempted to climb up and balance on them. He couldn't at first, but then wobbled along. "It would appear some people might be better at this than others. I just might fall and break my neck trying to explain the proper way to get on them and walk."

Everyone laughed, watching him try to explain how to stay up on the stilts while losing his balance and jumping off. They couldn't wait until they got their chance to try it.

"In today's race, you will not only race North against South, but race state against state. We thought it would be interesting to see which state is best at this."

Teams looked at each other and smiled, thinking they had this one in the bag. The South was convinced it would win the trophy today too. The teams of the North were determined that wouldn't happen again.

"As you can see, we have enough stilts for everyone to try. You'll line up along the line and race down to the end of the field and walk back. Whichever team has everyone across the line first, wins. Oh, wait… I forgot to mention one small thing." He smiled like he had a big surprise for them. "To give you a little practice, just for fun, the first race will be girls against boys. Southern girls

will race against Southern boys while the North does the same. It should be a great match."

"All-right!" a bunch of boys said, high-fiving each other and acting kind of tough. They thought they were faster and better than the girls, and now was their chance to prove it. The girls had the opposite idea. How hard could it be to walk on stilts? Ranger Moore had a twinkle in his eyes and a smile on his face—remembering when he was a kid and racing girls.

"Okay, head on over to the field and let's answer the question once and for all: who are the best stilt racers—girls or boys?" The words were hardly out of his mouth when every fifth grader ran toward the stilts.

"Bekka, help me up on these things," Hannah said, trying to get her balance and walk. They had five minutes to practice before the race started. Bekka didn't have any trouble getting up on hers and began walking in circles. She stopped long enough to explain it to her friend.

"It's easy—put your left foot on first, hop up and put your right foot on really fast. Then just start moving."

Soon Hannah got the hang of it and walked over to Stephen, who kept falling off because he tried to take too big of steps.

"How do you do that so good?"

"Easy—you just have to be a girl." Hannah laughed and headed back to Bekka who was near the starting line.

Ranger Moore blew his whistle. "Time's up. Most of you look like experts. Let's get this race underway. You will begin at the starting line, walk on your stilts down to the end of the field, go around the cannon that is in your lane, and come back to this starting point.

"I'll give you a hint on how to keep your rhythm as you walk. Back in the Civil War, many of the young boys and soldiers did not know how to tell their left foot from their right foot when they marched. Their commanding officer would call out 'right foot, left foot,' but they didn't know which foot was right or left. So someone came up with the idea of putting straw in the left shoe, and hay in the right shoe since they could tell the difference between hay and straw. When they marched, someone called out 'hay foot, straw foot,' and they marched together. If you want to help your teammate keep rhythm as they walk on their stilts, chant, 'hay foot, straw foot,' and maybe it will help."

Everyone got up on their stilts and waited for Ranger Moore to start the contest. He looked left at one team and right at the other. "On your mark, get set, go!"

More than one person started out too fast and fell off, slowing down their team. Some moved like jackrabbits while others moved like tortoises, not wanting to lose their balance. Bekka and Hannah had no problem doing it; neither did Ben and his friends. It was a neck and neck race almost to the end when the final boy crossed the line first and the hollering began. The girls wanted a do-over because a boy crossed over into their lane knocking a girl off, but Ranger Moore moved on to the big race of the North against the

South. He had them get with their teams and line up. What a test for their balance.

"Racers, are you ready? On your mark, get set, go!" Cheers and screams for team members were heard all over the field. Racers walked as fast as they could to make up time after falling off their stilts. Others made it down and around the cannon easily. None wanted to lose. Everyone wanted to win. The best racers were saved for the end, and competed as fast as they could.

Evan from Georgia made up a great deal of time so the South thought they had another victory. He crossed the line just as the last one from their team took off. Stephen crossed the line in his lane two steps after that, giving Ethan the last leg of the race for the North. It took every ounce of strength he had to make up the distance between him and the Southern racer. He wanted to take bigger steps but knew it would spell disaster if he did. "Stay calm, steady as you go," he told himself. It didn't look good for him.

The Southern racer was just faster and more sure-footed. Girls were jumping up and down screaming his name. Bekka had taken her turn, so was taking pictures of him while Hannah kept her camera on Ethan. Just as the Southern racer looked up to see how far he had to go, his stilt went into a hole in the ground. Over he went. He tried to get back up on the stilts but just couldn't overtake Ethan, who managed to step across the line seconds before him.

"We won! We won!" Hannah and Bekka screamed, as they took one last picture of the two boys. Both boys collapsed on the ground as they crossed the finish line.

This time, the students from the South stood around stunned at their loss.

Chapter 16

After lunch, Stephen and Ben got out the metal detector to hunt for the missing jacks and General Farnsworth's ring. A thorough search of all tents and bags had been made by the teachers to see if someone had taken Stephen's jacks and hid them in their tent. They were nowhere to be found.

With regret, Ranger Moore told Stephen he would have to keep his rule that a student couldn't play if they didn't have their own jacks, so the boys decided to recheck all the places they had been the night before. They waved the metal detector over every square inch of grass from their tent up to the flagpole, but nothing made it buzz faster.

Standing at the entrance of his tent, they heard Ethan yelling, "My jacks are missing! Somebody took my jacks!"

They couldn't believe their ears. More jacks were gone. They ran toward Ethan's tent; Ben arrived first and started quizzing his friend. "Did you take them out of your tent last night to hide them in the grass?"

"Yes, but I found them and put them back in my bag on my table. My bag is still there, but not my jacks. Just like what happened to Stephen."

It was rather suspicious that in each case, the jacks were missing but the bag was left on the table. They took the metal

detector into the tent and turned it on to see if someone was playing a prank on him by putting the jacks elsewhere out of sight.

The detector buzzed when it got near the zipper on Ethan's sleeping bag and then when it detected a jackknife in his duffel bag, but that was all. They waved it under the cots. No jacks!

Stephen was hopeful and offered one last suggestion.

"Let's do this around all the tents and see if they are there. If we don't find your jacks, we'll have to tell Ranger Moore."

Starting with the boys' tents, they went around every single one. Finding nothing, they moved on to the area by the girls' tents. Time was running out and they were getting desperate for answers. They knew what was missing but not who, how, why and when.

"Good afternoon, boys, whatcha doing?" asked the laundry lady, who was taking clean washcloths and water into each tent. After a hot day, a cool cloth felt good before bed.

"We're looking for..." All of a sudden the metal detector started buzzing like a beehive.

The three boys stopped dead in their tracks and started searching the grass for anything metal. They looked for small holes that might have jacks hidden in them, but not a one was found. They turned on the metal detector again, but it didn't make a sound. What happened?

"Hey, what are you doing?" Bekka asked, kneeling beside Ben in the grass. After taking dozens of pictures of teachers in

their old dresses and bonnets, she needed new batteries for her camera. She was most impressed with Mrs. Ranes' dress that looked like she had a hula hoop under it and couldn't resist taking a picture of the petticoat that had curved rods in it to keep it sticking out.

"We're looking for Ethan's jacks," Ben said. "Somebody took his too."

"What?" Her voice raised a few decibels.

"Keep your voice down," her brother told her. He didn't want anyone to hear what they were doing.

"How come you're over here by the girls' tents?"

"We looked all over by the boys' tents but they aren't in the grass there, so came here, and all of a sudden, the metal detector started going off. We dug and felt all over, but didn't find anything, and now it isn't buzzing fast anymore."

"Wow."

"Yeah, and now Ethan can't play jacks if he can't find his." Ben was getting upset with the situation. Who would be next? Bekka wondered the same thing and went into her tent to check for hers.

"B-E-N!"

When Bekka screamed, Ben knew she must be missing something, too. He dashed inside her tent.

"What's wrong?" he asked, somewhat in shock.

Bekka was standing on her cot with her hand over her mouth. Her eyes were bulging out of her head, and tears were almost ready to fall. She pointed downward.

The boys got the message to look under her cot. When they did, they jumped back! Lying up against the side of the tent was the skin of a snake. They couldn't believe their eyes. A snake had shed its skin right under Bekka's cot.

"Co-ol," the boys said together.

"No, it's creepy! Ben, get it out of here!" She was just about hysterical. "It must have been in here last night!"

Insects and reptiles usually didn't bother her, but to think a snake was slithering under her bed while she slept was just too much. Bekka sat down on her sleeping bag, brought her knees up to her chin, hid her face in her knees, and cried from fright.

Ben took charge. “Let’s look around and see if it’s still in here. Be careful, Stephen, it might be coiled up under something.” He knew snakes are cold-blooded and lie on warm things to absorb heat.

Just thinking about the possibility of a snake being under her or Hannah’s pillows made Bekka let out another half-scream. Her imagination went crazy!

“It wasn’t here yesterday when we came or I would have seen it.” She couldn’t stop thinking about when it might have come into their tent or worse yet—that it might have crawled over her in the night.

The boys carefully lifted the few things the girls brought with them, but didn’t find the snake. Ben tried to console his sister.

“It probably shed its skin and slithered out to the field. Maybe it liked the warmth of the tent this morning, and is gone now that it’s hot. Where’s your information book about snakes? We need to look at the pictures and compare them to the design on its dried skin.”

Bekka pointed downward again, under the cot. Her brother pulled out her suitcase and found the book lying on top. She had a bookmark at the Gettysburg pages. Ben read until he found the names of snakes.

“There are five kinds of snakes: garter and black rat snakes which are non-venomous, copperhead and timber rattlesnakes

that are poisonous, and the northern water snake that looks like it's poisonous, but isn't."

Bekka shuddered once again, wondering which kind of snake skin was under her cot. "Which do you think it is?"

Ben lay on his stomach and reached his hand over to grab it. "I'll pull it out and get a good look at it."

"Ben, be careful," she shrieked. She was really freaking out. "You don't know if the snake is somewhere watching you." She was not convinced it had slithered away.

"It's not here. We're making too much noise."

"Good!"

"Look, the design of the snake is on the skin." Ben compared it to the pictures in the book. Stephen crowded in to look at the pictures of the snakes. "I think it's a black rat snake. Good thing for you, Bekka, it's not a poisonous one."

Bekka groaned and hid her face in her knees, "Get it out of here! It's too creepy!"

Since Bekka couldn't bring herself to do it, Ben made an offer he usually didn't make. "Mom and Dad aren't going to believe you had a snake in your tent. We have to take a picture of it here by your cot. This thing has to be about four feet long," he said positioning it right in front of Bekka's suitcase. He reached for her camera. "I'll take the picture for you." He got a couple of good pictures and gave the camera back to Bekka.

"Let's take this over to our tent, Stephen. I think—no, I know—Hannah would freak out even more than Bekka if she ever saw it."

"Oh, yeah, she'd scream bloody murder," Stephen agreed. "Gotta get it out of here." The boys each grabbed an end of the snakeskin, and got up to leave.

BOOM! The cannon signaled time for the next round of games. Bekka's heart just wasn't in it.

Ben tried to make her feel better. "Since we didn't find Ethan's jacks, we have to report them missing too. I have an idea, but first, we'll put this in our tent. What if someone did this as a prank on you two girls, just to get you to be too scared to play jacks? We'll figure this out somehow."

Chapter 17

Ben and Stephen put the snake in their right hands and walked in single file back to their tent, acting like nothing unusual was dangling between them. Luckily for them, no one noticed or questioned what they had or where they found it. Their field trip was getting more bizarre by the day. They tucked the snake skin behind Ben's duffel bag under his cot. If someone came in, they wouldn't see it. To be honest, they did wonder when the snake crawled into the girls' tent and if it crawled over Bekka in the night. Even they would have been creeped out had it happened to them.

Bekka, glad to be rid of the snake skin, grabbed her jacks and ran out of the tent, in case—well, she just couldn't think about it. It would be a long, long time before that snakeskin was out of her head.

Ranger Moore was quite surprised to hear the boys report a second set of jacks missing. It raised another red flag in his head. The ranger was becoming more and more convinced someone was doing something to sabotage the Michigan boys' chances of winning. Ben offered to give Ethan his jacks to use during the afternoon games.

"Do you really want to forfeit so Ethan can use your jacks?"

"Yes," Ben continued, explaining. "I'll hang out with Stephen and we'll keep looking for his grandfather's ring. Maybe the jacks will show up somewhere."

"If that's your decision, then I'll go along with it."

The ranger signaled everyone to follow him inside to a large room where he would give new instructions.

"Is anyone else missing their jacks? We have a second person who found their bag empty, lying on the table in their tent." He paused to look around the room and waited for a response. "If any of you hear or see anything suspicious, please come to me. It isn't fair that innocent players are involved in this situation. If no one else is missing their jacks, we'll begin."

He explained Jacks was a game played by boys and girls alike, testing their hand and eye coordination. Some of the girls had played before and felt confident they had this one mastered.

Ranger Moore had everyone sit down on the floor and watch another ranger demonstrate how it was done. She dropped her handful of jacks and then threw her ball up into the air. Before it bounced, she scooped up a jack and caught the ball. She did it a second time and scooped up two jacks, and so on until they were all scooped up. Then the students were given time to practice. It was more challenging than walking on stilts. Balls rolled around the room and kids chased after them. Girls were definitely better than boys at this game, but for the sake of winning the trophy, they kept trying. Ranger Moore whistled, signaling it was time for each one to meet their match.

Meanwhile, Stephen knew which fields his great-great… grandfather had been at while in Gettysburg, so he and Ben got permission to go to Little Round Top with Mr. Dupries.

"After all these years, it would be amazing if you came across your great-great...grandfather's ring," their teacher commented.

"Yeah, we're hoping my metal detector can tell if something is a couple inches down in the dirt," Stephen stated, fingering the handle of his tool. Mr. Dupries admired their desire to keep looking.

"It is puzzling that things are coming up missing. I'm hoping your detector works for you because I want it to work for me. No one but the ranger knows, but last night during game time, someone took my Swiss army knife off the table in my tent. It was extra special in that it had lots of built-in gadgets which are useful when we are camping and I need a small tool."

Ben and Stephen's jaws dropped and their eyes popped wide open as their teacher told his story. It was more than puzzling. It confirmed their suspicions that someone was targeting their group. But who and why?

Once they were there, they wasted no time turning on the metal detector. They had a lot of ground to cover before it was time to go back to make dinner. After a half hour, Stephen's arms got tired so Ben took over and waved it left and right. To give him a break, Mr. Dupries took a turn. Getting near to the last acre, Stephen took the detector back, wanting to be the one to find it. Maybe, just maybe he would be successful.

Right at three o'clock, Mrs. Hopewell clanked on an old metal triangle, signaling the afternoon cooks to begin preparing dinner. With no sign of a knife, jacks or the ring, Ben and Stephen stopped looking and went over to the cooking area. Mr. Dupries decided to

circle back around by the Visitor's Center to keep looking in the grass. If someone was playing a prank on their team, they were doing a great job.

Just for the fun of it, as Ben and Stephen got near Mrs. Hopewell's pots and pans in the cooking area, they turned on the metal detector. The cast iron pan Ben had on his head that morning made it go crazy. The noise startled Mrs. Hopewell and her helpers, but Stephen pumped the air with his fists in excitement. He thought maybe his detector had somehow lost its sensitivity to metal.

"Yay, it still works!"

Ben recognized the laundry lady as she came to collect the wet towels Mrs. Hopewell had in a stack on a table. Noticing the metal detector in Stephen's hand she asked, "Hi, boys. Still lookin' for things?"

"Yeah," Ben replied. "Stephen lost his jacks and his great-great-great-grandfather lost his wedding ring somewhere around here in the Civil War, so we're hoping we can find them or maybe something else really old."

As if to prove what he was saying, the metal detector started clicking like crazy. The boys turned it off and began looking all around for something that might have caused it to buzz. They pushed down on the ground, even parting the grass in their frantic search for a metal object, but nothing was there.

"This is so strange," Ben moaned in frustration. "It went off when we got near the pans and then went off when we weren't around anything." Stephen was getting frustrated too.

Mrs. Hopewell looked at her watch. "Okay, boys, please put that away, and let's get going on this meal. You wanted to do something difficult, well, this is it. We're having what is known as Mulligan stew and President Lincoln's favorite apple pie. And it's all going to be baked in Mr. Adams' trench," she said, pointing to the teacher who had a shovel in his hand. Another eye-popping, jaw-dropping experience.

Chapter 18

Mr. Adams, the teacher from Georgia, was working up a sweat digging a trench eight inches deep. This method of cooking dinner was totally new to the students.

Ben couldn't help but ask, "Are you serious? We're going to cook dinner in the dirt?"

"Yes, Ben, we're cooking dinner in that trench in pots which will lie on a bed of coals."

Mrs. Hopewell started her instructions. "Now, this may look unusual to you, but back in the 1860s when they didn't have a cook stove available, they used the ground as an oven. As you can see, Mr. Adams dug us a perfect trench to cook in. Now, let's get a fire going! Boys, please put these briquettes in the trench and Mr. Adams will set them on fire," she said, handing one of the boys a large bag of charcoal. "During the Civil War, they burned sticks and other things, but for our meal today, we'll use charcoal since Ranger Moore didn't give us permission to cut down one of their trees." She laughed at that idea.

Mrs. Hopewell walked over to the cook table. "Girls, you begin working on the food. The boys will join us when they are done. Let me see your name tags so I don't get mixed up. I've seen so many names, I can't keep everyone straight. Hannah, you begin peeling potatoes and Bekka, you peel carrots. We need about forty of each. You two girls from Georgia, please help them. Peelers are

in that bin over there. I'll work on the meat as it takes an extra sharp knife to cut it. If no one has any questions, let's get going."

As the girls peeled, the boys ripped open the bag of charcoal and worked to lay out an even amount along the whole trench.

"This is cool," Ben said, convinced they should try it sometime. He was doubtful his mother would let him dig a trench in their backyard, but maybe they could try it at a campground someday.

When it appeared they had a good amount of charcoal in the trench, Mr. Adams lit the coals with matches. The boys jumped back as flames flew up. This was sure different than a gas grill at home.

Mrs. Hopewell watched as the girls peeled the biggest pile of vegetables they'd ever seen. Mr. Adams came over to cut them into bite-size pieces.

"Great job, everyone," said Mrs. Hopewell, inspecting the huge bowl of potatoes and carrots. "Boys, there are six pots over there on that table. Please get them and bring them here for us to fill."

Off they went to retrieve them. Ben spied the metal detector and wanted to turn it on again, but resisted the urge. He didn't want to interrupt Mrs. Hopewell who was giving instructions for assembling the meal.

"To make perfect Mulligan stew, you put your meat chunks on the bottom of the pan. They take the longest to cook, so they need to be near the coals."

None of the students had ever handled chunks of raw meat with a fork before. While the girls carefully put the fork into each piece and laid them into the pan, the boys saw it as a good time to act out a scene from a pirate movie.

"Ahoy, matey," Ben declared to Stephen, swinging his long handled fork like a sword. "Argh, what a fine piece of flesh you have on your dagger."

"Fine piece of flesh, indeed," his friend replied.

Ben waved a piece of meat under Bekka's nose. "Aye, me pretty, care to dine with me this fine evening?"

"Ben, you're being gross. Don't touch my face with that. You know Mom says you shouldn't touch raw meat!"

"I know, but this is the 1860s when pirates lived and no one knew about germs."

"If you don't quit, I'm telling on you."

Chapter 19

Mrs. Hopewell observed Ben's clowning around. She liked his spirit, but she also knew girls didn't like raw meat put in their faces. It was time to get the show on the road.

"Are we eating this tonight or tomorrow, you two? I don't want a mutiny here at Gettysburg. As they say, 'an army runs on its stomach,' and this is the biggest army of hungry youngsters I've seen in a long time. If you have your meat in your pots, grab handfuls of potatoes and carrots, and put them on top. There are cans of tomato juice on that table. Each of you open a can, and pour it in. Shake on a little salt and pepper, add a pitcher of water, and put on a lid. Mr. Adams will put them down in the trench on the hot coals."

While the students filled their pans with meat and vegetables, Mrs. Hopewell thought she'd tell them a cooking story they would remember for a long time.

"I want you to imagine a meal similar to this being prepared in the White House. These are all foods you enjoy eating. Well, back in the 1800s, shooting squirrels and cooking them in Squirrel Soup was common, and people enjoyed eating it. President Lincoln grew up in Kentucky and Illinois and undoubtedly ate squirrel."

"Ew-ww," the girls exclaimed. Squirrels ran around their yards and none of them could imagine their fathers catching a squirrel or their mothers cooking it for dinner.

"We treat them like a backyard pet but back then, they were meat in the pot."

Hannah had a shocked look on her face. "I'm glad I didn't live back then. I'd never eat a squirrel."

"Did they eat snakes back then?" Stephen asked. Bekka gave him the evil-eye look which dared him to make a wise crack about her freaking out in the tent.

"I'm sure they did. Several years ago at a restaurant called The Rooftop Landing, I had fried rattlesnake. It didn't taste too bad—it tasted like chicken."

"How can they cook a snake? It would be too long to fit in a pan," Bekka asked, shuddering once more. Visions of four feet of snake coiled in a cooking pot almost caused a scream to escape.

On the other hand, Mrs. Hopewell laughed while imagining someone coiling up a long snake in a frying pan. "They cut it up into pieces. Would you ever eat it?"

"No, never!" was all she could say. She remembered what the boys said about not scaring Hannah, so didn't explain her outburst.

When all of the pots were filled with meat and vegetables, Mr. Adams lowered them into the trench. The junior cooks were proud of their 1860s meal and hoped it tasted as good as Mrs. Hopewell promised.

"While your Mulligan stew masterpieces are cooking in the trench, we'll make our pies. President Lincoln loved a good apple

pie. Can all of you use a paring knife safely? Your mothers wouldn't understand if you came home missing your fingertips. I want to teach you something that people in the 1860s tried to do each time they peeled an apple."

She took a clean apple in her left hand and started peeling very close to the top of the apple. All eyes were on her knife as it moved slowly and smoothly in a circular motion.

"Back then, they tried to peel an apple without breaking the skin. They could peel it around the whole thing without stopping or breaking it off." As she peeled, the length of the skin got longer and longer. It amazed everyone that she could do it.

"Want to try it?"

"Yeah," and "yes, ma'am," they answered.

"It's kind of a challenge to go around without stopping, but as I showed you, go slowly and be very careful with your paring knife. You don't want to take off your skin with the peeling or stab the palm of your hand." She sliced her apple and put it in a huge bowl.

Peeling an apple without breaking the skin was much harder than it looked. No one but Mrs. Hopewell was successful at it. Some had skin two or three inches long but not seven or eight inches like hers. Ben and Stephen began eating their apple skins as they broke off. The more they peeled, the more they ate, until they were getting full.

“I wonder if Johnny Appleseed tried this,” Mr. Adams said, showing off his peeling which looked to be about five inches long. “With all his apples, I bet he was pretty good at this.”

Just then, Rachel from Georgia jumped and ducked her head. “Mrs. Hopewell, I think a bee just flew into the apples!”

Chapter 20

Mrs. Hopewell wiped her hands on her apron and reached for the bowl. Rachel took three giant steps backward.

"Did you really see a bee go into the apples? Where?" Mrs. Hopewell turned the bowl around so she could get a better look at where Rachel pointed. "Bees love anything sweet like fresh apples. I'll keep looking for it while you all get going on the pie crusts." *This is not supposed to happen,* she thought, as she fished the bee out and sent it on its way. Time was running out.

"How many of you have ever made a pie crust before? It isn't hard to mix it together, but it's tricky getting it rolled out and into the pie dish. Who has ever used a measuring cup or measuring spoons before?"

Only one hand went up—Bekka's. "Oh boy, I can see we are in for a cooking lesson," Mrs. Hopewell said, reaching for her measuring utensils.

"When you cook, make sure you read the handles on these utensils carefully to see what size they are. When a recipe says to put in one-half cup or one-half teaspoon, make sure you have the right size. You don't want to put in one-half cup of salt when it says to put in one-half teaspoon. That would taste nasty."

The girls giggled, and the boys stuck out their tongues and pretended to gag.

“Oh, and another thing—read your recipe and follow the order it tells you to put things in the bowl–don’t just dump it all on top of each other. In some cases, you’d end up with a mess and globs.” She reached for the flour, shortening, and salt. “Let’s get measuring our ingredients.”

Mrs. Hopewell forgot to mention to measure flour slowly, and within seconds, there was a flour shower, coating everyone’s faces, hair and arms with white dust.

“My, you kids have aged right before my eyes!” she declared.

The boys saw this as a great opportunity to add a bit more flour to the shower, and when Mrs. Hopewell wasn’t looking, Evan from Georgia threw a handful toward the boys from Michigan, and a white dust storm blew through the cooking area. They looked like ghosts, and couldn’t help but crack up laughing.

“Boys!” Mrs. Hopewell looked and sounded shocked. “What in the world?” She just couldn’t help laughing herself. “Somebody needs a picture of this.”

“Wait,” Bekka said, grabbing her camera. “Hold still. This will be perfect for the poster at school.” Hannah was disappointed she had left her camera in the tent and couldn’t take a picture too.

“Alright, back to the crust,” Mrs. Hopewell said after the boys posed for the picture of the day. “If your flour, shortening, and salt are mixed in your bowls, let’s roll out the dough.” This was one cooking lesson she’d never forget! But, it wasn’t over and there were more antics.

Too late, she realized she should never have given rolling pins to fifth grade boys. They suddenly turned them into dueling weapons and pie baking came to a halt again. The girls watched and rolled their eyes. Mrs. Hopewell almost gave up.

"Boys, remember, we don't have ovens here; we have to cook these pies down in those trenches, too. If we don't get cracking, we'll be eating pies for breakfast."

"Sounds good to me!" Ben stated. He liked pies no matter what time of day they were served.

"Back in the 1860s they rolled pie crusts out on a floured surface. I'm almost afraid to suggest you sprinkle more flour on the table. Since we have had several delays, I'm going to teach you a handy-dandy time-saver for when you make pies for your families."

"Yeah, like that's going to happen," said Rachel from Georgia. "I'm busy playing sports after school and on Saturdays. Maybe my mama would let me make pies instead of doing my homework."

"Yeah, like that's going to happen," Mrs. Hopewell repeated back to her, chuckling as she began to form her dough into a ball. "Take a little more than half of your dough and make a ball. Don't handle it too much; we want flaky crusts." She watched to see that everyone's ball of dough was about equal to the others.

Holding up a roll of plastic wrap, she said, "To make it a lot easier on you, I'll give each of you two pieces of this wrap. Lay one on the table and put your ball in the middle. Put the other piece of wrap on top, and push down with your hand."

Everyone watched carefully and then followed her directions. "Now, take your rolling pin, start in the middle of the ball, and work outward towards the edges, applying pressure as you push. Turn it every so often, as you make a circle. Because the wrap is plastic, the dough won't stick to your rolling pin. And you'll be able to flip it into the pan with great success."

"No way. Wait 'til you show this to Mom," Ben said to his sister, who was well on her way to making a great-looking pie crust. "This stuff is amazing."

Chapter 21

To everyone's amazement, the junior bakers were soon ready to move to the next step. Mrs. Hopewell was impressed. "Your circles look big enough to put in the pie dish. Carefully pull off the top layer of your plastic wrap." One by one, they did it and everyone was proud of their crust.

"Now, put your hands under the bottom layer of plastic wrap and take your crust and lift it up over your pie dish. Move one hand underneath to the center of the crust and put your right hand on the top of the crust to steady it. Carefully flip your crust upside down into the pie dish and pull off the plastic wrap."

"Wow! I did it," boasted Ben, who was totally surprised it didn't flip off onto the ground.

"Me too. It really works," squealed Bekka. "Ben, we have to try this at home. Mom will be amazed."

"Tah da! You did it!" Mrs. Hopewell beamed with pride at their success. "I think we will still have pies for dessert tonight!"

"Aw, I wanted apple pie cereal for breakfast," Ben joked.

"Yeah, me too," agreed Stephen.

"To make an impressive pie, you have to have lots of filling, so reach into the bowl and spoon out plenty of apples into your

pie dishes. Make them mountain high by peaking them up in the middle."

Mrs. Hopewell should have known the boys would try to make king-of-the-mountain high pies. They piled apples so high, they were falling off the edges of the dish. She just shook her head.

"I'm not sure if it is safe to have you make a crust to cover your monster pies," she remarked, but handed out more crust to roll out.

Each one tried to outdo the others with their gigantic top crust circles, knowing it was going to take a lot of dough to cover them completely. The boys certainly tested Mrs. Hopewell's patience, but everyone was having a great time making their dessert.

Mr. Adams had a row of Dutch oven kettles on another table ready to set the pies into. Hot coals were already in the bottom of each pan to help the pies cook faster.

He lowered the pies into the pans and put the lids on and then set them in the trench on the hot charcoal briquettes to bake for an hour or more.

"I never saw a pie cook like this before," Hannah remarked, amazed that someone invented it.

Mrs. Hopewell bent over the trench inspecting each pot to be sure the lids were on tightly. "People had to be resourceful and do things like this when an oven wasn't available. Judging by the looks of these full pans, I'd say we're in for a finger-licking good meal!"

She stood up, wiped her hands on her apron, and declared the job "done." Usually she had students help wash dishes, but she could just imagine what the boys would do with a dishpan of sudsy water.

Glad to be back on the hunt for missing items, Ben and Stephen took off like two jackrabbits scared out of their hiding spot. The girls went to their tent to get Hannah's camera so she could go back and take pictures of the pots in the trench. Who could have known their fun afternoon would dissolve into more disasters?

Chapter 22

Within minutes, the boys saw Bekka and Hannah running toward them. Hannah was in tears.

"Somebody stole Hannah's camera," Bekka declared.

"What?" Ben asked, amazed another item was missing.

"Who is doing this and why?" Stephen asked, feeling bad for her. Remembering his missing jacks, he knew what it felt like to have something stolen. "Did you tell anybody yet?"

Hannah shook her head 'no' as she looked around for anyone holding a camera similar to hers.

"Let's go find Mr. Dupries. He's not going to believe that this happened again to someone from our class. He told us earlier that someone stole his Swiss army knife." The girls stopped dead in their tracks and did a double take at Stephen when he dropped that bombshell on them.

The four of them went in search of their teacher. They figured he was near the flagpole since the afternoon free time was about over and it was time for another competition with the South.

Sure enough, Bekka spotted him by the flagpole and pointed. "There he is. He's going to be really upset that more of our stuff is missing." Off they shot to tell him this bit of news.

"Mr. Dupries," Ben called out to him. "You aren't going to believe this. Hannah's camera is missing from their tent."

Ben was right. Their teacher couldn't believe it. "Are you sure you left it there?"

"Yes," Hannah half-whimpered, trying not to break down crying again. She had used her Christmas money to buy the camera, and her mother had told her not to lose it. "I didn't want to get it messy when we were cooking, so I left it on my table. When I went back to get it so I could take a picture of the pans in the trench, it was gone." Tears were really coming down.

"Let's go back and look again. I'll make a thorough search to be sure." Mr. Dupries was trying hard to make her feel better.

To no one's surprise, the camera was not to be found. The girls knew they had searched every inch of the tent, but Mr. Dupries had to be sure in case Ranger Moore asked him if he'd looked for it too.

"Anything else missing?" he asked.

"No, not that we can see," Bekka answered.

"Ranger Moore is not going to be pleased. It would appear someone from the other teams doesn't want us to do well in the games. This is a big distraction for you, Hannah. You'll be thinking about your camera being stolen rather than playing a game."

"Yeah, I just want to go search in all the tents until I find it." She was trying hard to sound strong.

“I don’t blame you. Let’s ask around and see if anyone saw someone entering your tent while you were cooking.”

Out in the play area, everyone they talked to was shocked at Hannah’s loss. Many volunteered to search each other’s tents to be sure someone wasn’t covering up the truth. Mr. Dupries went to tell Ranger Moore and he delayed having the cannon fired until a search of the tents was complete. Students from the South kept saying they weren’t responsible and were willing to open all their bags to prove it. The camera just couldn’t be found anywhere.

BOOM! Ranger Moore had the cannon go off to get everyone’s attention and have them gather at the flagpole to discuss this new development.

Chapter 23

“Something is going on here and we plan to get to the bottom of it sooner or later. Two sets of jacks are missing, now Hannah’s camera, and many of you are not aware, but Mr. Dupries’ Swiss army knife was stolen last evening during game time.”

Wide-eyed kids looked at each other. This was major. Somebody was going to be in really big trouble.

“A Swiss army knife and a camera are not easy to hide, so someone is removing things from tents somehow unobserved. Once again, I want to remind you to not touch someone else’s property. Live by the Golden Rule and treat other people the way you’d want to be treated. None of us want to have our things stolen, so don’t be a thief and take anything that doesn’t belong to you.” He paused long enough for the silence to have an effect on the fifth graders and adults. Someone was intentionally spoiling their fun.

He took a deep breath and began talking in a happier tone of voice. “Okay, let’s get on to our afternoon game because I hear dinner is going to be extra special.”

Delicious smells from the cooking pots were floating through the air. Whistles and cheers went up for the cooks.

“I think this next game will not be new to you. Probably most of you have already played it but didn’t realize it is an old game.

It's called Nine Pins. So that you wouldn't see what was going on, I had rangers set up the game on the other side of the Visitor's Center. Follow me."

Off trooped one hundred thirty students and adults, single file, behind Ranger Moore. They felt like soldiers in the Civil War.

Much to their amazement, as they turned the corner on the walkway, it looked like they were at an outdoor bowling alley. Those who had bowled before figured they were going to do quite well and let it be known to those around them. Ranger Moore smiled at everyone's expressions.

"Nine Pins is very similar to our ten-pin bowling. Children in the 1860s used wooden balls to knock down wooden pins, very much like we do today. Except, it was played outside and grass makes it more difficult to knock them down. As with regular bowling, when it's your turn, you'll each get two tries to knock down the pins. Teachers will be counting pins and keeping score. Someone will be down by the pins setting them back up in the V-shape. We are still competing North against the South, so you will be matched South Carolina against Pennsylvania, New York against Georgia, and Michigan against Virginia. You will have smaller teams of ten per side and it will be the best two out of three games. You have five minutes to set up your teams and then I'll blow my whistle."

Teachers broke down their classes into three teams of ten and matched them up with ten members from the opposing state. Ben and Bekka hadn't met many from Virginia except Ashley and

C.P., so they guessed which ones might be good at Nine Pins. Their dad told them it was called 'sizing up the competition'. They didn't want any surprises, but it happened. Ashley looked like she couldn't roll a ball very far, but when she did, it went straight as an arrow, heading for the first pin every time. C.P. proved he was as good at bowling as he was at spitting watermelon seeds.

"I don't think the North stands a chance if everybody on their team is as good as they are." Bekka squirmed close to Ben, not wanting anyone else to hear her comment.

"Yeah, I think we are in for it again," he agreed. "Let's give it our best shot."

One by one the teams took turns, knocking down and then missing the pins. The boys seemed to be able to hit more of them,

but the girls put forth a little extra effort, and kept up quite well. It was neck and neck. Since there were no electric score keeping signs, no one but the teachers knew who was ahead. Kids from the North really wanted that traveling trophy to be on their side of the flagpole tonight, while kids from the South wanted to keep it right where it was—on their side. Everyone was having a great time. They wouldn't have been had they been able to see what was going on over in the tents.

Chapter 24

"This is too easy," one said as they neared the tents.

Silently they moved about, entering tent after tent, observing what was left out on tables. They were unstoppable. Not wanting to draw a great deal of attention to themselves, they decided to be selective in what they took from now on.

Voices of kids playing on the other side of the Visitor's Center assured them no one would be around for awhile. They didn't need any of the things they were taking. They just wanted to test their skills.

"You do these tents and I'll do those tents so it doesn't look suspicious," the younger one said, pointing out in the distance.

"Okay, but hurry, this is our last chance today."

Ten minutes later one met the other coming out of a tent. "Bingo—I got the deadliest catch yet. It's sweet. Let's go."

Together they walked into the Visitor's Center, smiling smugly, undetected after pulling off another theft.

"Yep, this is too easy."

Chapter 25

BOOM! The cannon blasted, ending the game of Nine Pins. Everyone was adjusting to the sound of the cannon blast and didn't startle quite as easily.

"I might go home deaf, but I'll know why," Ben said, just about yelling in Stephen's ear.

Stephen put his hand behind his ear, pretending not to hear well anymore. "Aye, sonny, what'd ya say?"

Keeping on with the charade that he couldn't hear well, Ben jokingly said, "I said I have a deaf fly."

"A dead fly? How'd your fly die?" Stephen kept the fun going.

"My fly didn't die, he just couldn't fly."

"Your fly couldn't fly; did he walk?"

"Flies can't talk; you hearing voices in your head?"

"Must be. The cannon blasts are driving me crazy."

"Oh, your fly didn't die, it was your ears."

Bekka listened to their crazy talk. She shook her head and walked away, wondering if they would ever grow up?

She headed to her tent to talk to Hannah who was still searching for her camera. Lifting up everything from every surface,

emptying out the contents of her suitcase, shaking out her sleeping bag, both girls became convinced the camera definitely was the possession of someone else.

"Why would someone want to take your camera?" Bekka asked one more time, not expecting an answer. She sat on her cot, her camera in hand. "I'm going to look at the pictures I've taken to make sure I have some of all the tents, fields, kids from the South and North in their old clothes, and the cooking area so if we can't find your camera, I can have copies made for your poster." She really did feel bad for her friend.

"Thanks," Hannah replied. She was devastated.

Bekka looked at the monitor in the back of her digital camera to review the pictures she had taken. There were a lot to go through. She had gone just past the ones of the snake when Hannah joined her on the cot to look at them too. Soon they were giggling at the crazy ones she took of kids chasing runaway hoops, boys colliding with each other trying to get the shuttlecocks, teachers having a hard time walking in their hooped skirts, teammates on the ground with stilts lying next to them, and the metal detector being the center of attention.

Bekka put her camera in its case and looked out the tent, thinking out loud. "It makes you wonder if we'll ever find out who is taking all this stuff and how is it they are not being noticed?"

"You have the mind of a detective, Bekka. Come on, think. Think hard. What is happening that we are overlooking? Why are people picking on just our class?"

From across the field by the tents from the South, she saw two boys running to their teacher, holding open a small box. The teacher talked to them for a minute and walked over to the boys' tent. Shortly, all three came back out and headed for the flagpole where Ranger Moore stood alongside Mrs. Hopewell who held the triangle dinner bell.

Just before she rang the bell, Bekka saw the teacher signal Mr. Moore, who stopped Mrs. Hopewell's hand. Bekka could tell he was getting upset as he listened.

"I think something happened at a boys' tent over there."

"How do you know?" Hannah asked, looking out too.

Bekka relayed what she had just witnessed, and together they casually walked toward the flagpole. To their surprise, it was Evan from Georgia talking to the ranger.

"Tell me again, son, what is missing?"

"Lures, my daddy's best lures he uses for fishing. I thought we would be fishing up here and I wanted to bring some prize-winning lures to catch me some big ones. My daddy's gonna be so mad I brought them. He's gonna be even more mad that someone stole them."

"We don't know for sure they were stolen," said Ranger Moore.

"Yes, I do. I just showed them to Monty after lunch and left the box on my table. I am in so much trouble." Evan was beginning to panic.

"Try to remain calm, son. We're working to find the person or persons responsible for creating this drama at our reenactment games. Mrs. Hopewell, please ring the bell, and let's eat dinner. I can't solve mysteries on an empty stomach."

Seeing Bekka, he asked her to please find Stephen and tell him his metal detector would be needed after dinner. She and Hannah didn't quit running 'til they found Stephen and blurted out the newsflash.

"You've got to be kidding! Mr. Moore wants me to look for something else that's gone missing?" Stephen was feeling rather important. He and Ben were about to go over to eat, so they grabbed the detector and took it with them. Sooner or later, it might just prove to be the best weapon against crime at this battlefield.

Chapter 26

"Tonight's dinner is brought to you by Michigan and Georgia," Ranger Moore announced. "It's Mulligan Stew and apple pie a la trench."

Everyone cheered because it smelled so good. Ranger Moore had them look at how it was cooked—eight inches down in the ground. Those who had not helped make the meal were shocked to see a trench with hot coals in it. Even the adults had never heard nor seen anything like it before.

"If you're ready for a gourmet meal, let's begin," Mrs. Hopewell said, especially proud of her work crew.

The junior cooks became the servers of the food. Their friends held out bowls to be filled with the stew and each one took a biscuit Mrs. Hopewell had made after she had dismissed her helpers earlier in the afternoon. She couldn't risk her biscuits becoming baseballs flying through the air in the hands of boys like Ben and Stephen, so she didn't ask for their help.

To the amazement of all, the stew tasted very good and many went back for seconds, and for the really hungry ones, thirds!

"I'm going to make this for my family when we go camping," Bekka declared. "I'm sure Dad will dig me a hole and I can show my parents how it's done. And I might even make a pie—without a flour shower." She looked directly at the boys. Ben and Stephen poked each other and laughed, remembering their ghostly white faces. They were just having fun—that's what boys do best.

Ranger Moore stood up to speak, a tall top hat on his head. "Four months after the battle of Gettysburg, President Lincoln came here to Gettysburg to help dedicate a military cemetery for soldiers. He was upset our country was divided over slavery and wanted the fighting to stop so that our country could become united again. Everyone thought he would give a long speech, but it was only two minutes long. He didn't have a speech writer, like a lot of presidents do these days, and he wrote it on the back of an envelope while riding on the train over from Washington. He didn't know people would memorize it or that it would become famous, calling it the Gettysburg Address, but it did. Hats off to President Lincoln who got his wish for our nation becoming united once

again." With that, Ranger Moore took off his hat and took a bow. People clapped and whistled.

He stepped over to the table filled with pies and took a good look at them. "For dessert tonight, we have mountain-high pies—one of President Lincoln's favorites. To make sure there is enough for all, it will be ladies before gentlemen."

"Awww," groaned a bunch of the boys. They hated that. The ranger was right though, not a crumb was left when the boys finished going through the line.

When he was finished eating, Ranger Moore went to the microphone and held up the traveling trophy. "Another great day of competition. Both sides showed great sportsmanship, and we have a winner. I will announce it tonight during our bonfire, after we make the all-time favorite late-night outdoor snack—s'mores.

"Yay! S'mores!" Ben cheered. "I like my marshmallows black."

"Oh, yuk. They have to be golden brown," a voice answered back. Many others agreed—with both boys.

"It's obvious, this camp is divided, even when it comes to roasting marshmallows. Go have fun until the bugler plays Taps at dusk. Then head over to the campfire for songs and s'mores."

As everyone got up to leave, Ranger Moore asked Ben and Stephen to stay behind. Bekka and Hannah wanted to hear what the ranger had to say, but decided they shouldn't stay, so walked back to their tent. Bekka would drag the information out of Ben later.

"Boys, it would appear some fishing lures have been taken from Evan's tent on the South's side," Ranger Moore admitted, rubbing his chin with his thumb and first finger.

"Wow," both boys said in unison.

"I've been doing some thinking as to who could have been snooping in the tents during Nine Pins. No one comes to mind, so would you please help me out one more time and go search the field all around the South's end of the camp?"

"Ranger Moore, what does a lure look like?" Stephen asked, not having seen one before.

"Lures are used for fishing. They're metal, kind of oblong in shape and are about three inches long. They have a hook on one end and sometimes decorative feathers on the other. They lure fish to the hook. Evan told me they were gold and green, so they won't be very noticeable in the grass. Just be careful of the hook; you don't want to get a nasty scratch or get it hooked in a finger."

"We'll be careful," Stephen assured Ranger Moore.

"Should you find them, please bring them directly to me."

"We will," Ben promised.

Off they went with the metal detector in hand. This field trip was going to be one for the record books. They were smack dab right in the middle of a crime scene and were being asked to help find the evidence and possibly lead the ranger to the crook or crooks. After an hour of searching, they quit.

"I think we need some back-up help to solve this," Ben declared. He knew Bekka had a good head for thinking things through and wanted to talk to her about this new development. Somehow between them, they could come up with a pattern of how the thefts were happening.

"Let's get the girls in on this with us."

"Good idea," Ben's buddy replied.

Chapter 27

"You're right, there has to be a pattern here which just isn't jumping out at us," Bekka said, squinting her eyes as she put her hand under her chin. She did that when she was deep in thought. Stephen and Ben stared into space.

"Let's think about what we already know," Bekka began. "First of all, Stephen's jacks came up missing. They were on the table and disappeared in the afternoon when we were playing hoop and sticks. Second, Ethan's jacks came up missing when we were playing marbles. Every student had to play or forfeit, so we can conclude it wasn't a student who took it during a game."

"Unless it was someone who came back for a camera or maybe a visor," Hannah interjected.

"Well, maybe, but it would have been pretty risky for them to go into someone's tent when that person or a ranger might have been watching," Bekka replied.

Ben brought up something else. "When do you think someone dared go into Mr. Dupries' tent? That was gutsy. And it looked as though our class was the target, but now the South has had something stolen too. So, it must be someone who doesn't care who wins or loses, or someone who wants to throw us off the track in our thinking."

“What’s really weird,” Stephen cut in, “is that nothing has shown up in anyone’s suitcases or sleeping bags. It’s like they are vanishing in thin air. Bekka, do you see anything in any of your pictures that might give you any clues?”

“No. And I’ve looked at them two or three times. There must be something I am missing.”

“It would be so cool to set a trap and see if someone falls for it,” Ben suggested. “If any of you have any good ideas, let’s talk about it later. Ranger Moore wanted us to use the metal detector over all the grass area before the bonfire. My arms are rested so we can keep going.”

“Hannah and I decided we’d go over to the Nurse’s Station tonight,” Bekka informed the boys. “I want to see how nurses treated people in the 1860s when they were sick.”

“Be my guest,” Ben said. “Personally, I, as your twin brother, don’t like the sight of blood, mine included. I think I feel faint.” He grimaced and held his head—pretending to be ill.

After the boys left, Bekka changed into her nurse’s uniform. She wanted to observe their school nurse, Mrs. Haynie, in action. Fortunately, there hadn’t been any broken or sprained bones, so she didn’t think Mrs. Haynie would be in the middle of a medical emergency. Maybe she and Hannah could sterilize some medical instruments and put them on a tray in case someone came in needing attention. Bekka grabbed her costume nurse’s cap and camera so Hannah could take a picture of her with Mrs. Haynie.

“If somebody is in there getting stitches, I’m leaving,” Hannah informed her as they approached the medical tent. “I’m with your brother. I don’t like the sight of blood. I know I would faint.”

“It doesn’t bother me like snakes do.” All of a sudden Bekka bit her lip and stopped talking.

Hannah noticed the change in her voice and looked at her friend. “When did you see a snake?”

“Uh.” She didn’t make eye contact with Hannah.

“Bekka, did you see a snake when I wasn’t around?”

“Well, maybe.”

“You didn’t tell me because you knew I’d freak out, right?”

Bekka was spared having to tell the truth as Mrs. Haynie came to the door of the tent just then.

“Hi, girls, you hurt?”

“No, we just wanted to see what a medical tent looks like and offer to help with anything,” Bekka replied.

Mrs. Haynie seemed pleased the girls had an interest in her profession. “Don’t you look cute in your uniform, Bekka! Any chance you want to be a nurse someday?”

“Maybe. My aunt works in a hospital. She thinks I would make a good nurse since I don’t faint at the sight of blood.” She emphasized the word faint and looked at Hannah.

"That's definitely helpful, especially if there's an emergency and someone needs stitches. Want to have a look around? Everything has been sterilized, so please don't touch any of my medical instruments. Back in the 1860s they didn't have the medicines and knowledge we do now, but they discovered things we have learned from. Let me give you a tour and you can see what is in the many colored bottles I have here."

Bekka listened so intently she was surprised when Hannah took her picture with Mrs. Haynie, who was also in an old-fashioned nurse's uniform. Bekka wondered how ladies could stand wearing long dresses in the summer heat. Just as they were about to leave, a woman rushed into the Nurse's Station with a nasty scratch on her ankle.

"What happened to you?" Mrs. Haynie asked, bending over to get a closer look. "It's bleeding quite badly. Let me see if it's going to need a few stitches."

She began putting pressure on the cut to stop the bleeding, then lifted the cloth and looked again at the ankle. "We're going to need some antiseptic to clean it out. Being out here on these battlefields, you could get infection from a number of things. Can you tell me what happened?"

"Uh, I, uh, a knife scraped it when it fell out of my hand."

"A knife? It must have fallen at a strange angle to scrape your leg like this."

The woman seemed to be very nervous, looking all around the tent instead of looking at Mrs. Haynie.

Hannah wanted a picture of Mrs. Haynie performing a medical procedure so took a couple of them from back by the doorway.

"Girls, I think it would be good if you left now while I work on... I don't think I know your name."

"Sonya Truce."

"Sonya," Mrs. Haynie repeated. "I think I need some privacy to work on her leg. You can come back another time and we'll finish our tour of the tent. Bye."

Bekka wanted to stay and watch Sonya get stitches, but knew it was time to leave. As they left, they heard Mrs. Haynie ask her how long ago it happened. It sounded like Sonya said four hours ago. No wonder it was red, it was getting infected in this heat. Good thing Mrs. Haynie came on the trip, Bekka thought.

They spotted the boys still searching the ground over by the Southern tents, so trotted off to join them in their search for the lures. Try as hard as they could, Ben and Stephen didn't locate anything metal in the whole camp area. Apparently, whoever took the fishing lures out of the box in Evan's tent took them with them.

The boys called off their search and went back to their tent to put the metal detector away. It was nearly dark and time for the campfire and s'mores. This mystery was going unsolved—for now.

Chapter 28

Ranger Moore and a group of boys were building a roaring fire when the bugler started playing Taps, the official song played at the end of a day. Millions of stars shone in the dark night sky—much more visibly than Ben and Bekka saw in Lansing where city lights prevent a good view of faraway stars.

A man with a guitar stepped forward and told of the songs soldiers from the North and the South sang as they marched. Songs like "The Battle Hymn of the Republic", "Dixie", "Yankee Doodle", and "Swanee River". He asked if anyone knew them. Some raised their hands, but most didn't. Teachers knew all of them, so he had a drummer come up to play with him while the crowd sang. It made them feel like they were living back in 1863, far, far from home.

The best part of the evening was when Ranger Moore announced it was time for s'mores. Tables were filled with long-handled skewers, marshmallows, chocolate bars and graham crackers. Ben and Bekka were shocked to see kids raise their hands when asked if they had never made one before. For their benefit, Ranger Moore did a demonstration.

"The proper way to make a s'more is to first rip open a bag of marshmallows. To test whether they are good or bad, take two and pop them into your mouth. If you can chew them, they're good." Laughter broke out all around. Ranger Moore was

usually a serious person, but not when he was around a bag of marshmallows.

"Seriously though, when you're done swallowing those marshmallows, take two more and put them on your skewer and hold it over the fire. A word of caution—it's dark out, so be very careful walking with a skewer. Keep them low to the ground, not up near faces." As he talked, he demonstrated moving his skewer up and down, mainly pointing it toward the ground.

"You roast your marshmallows in the fire to whichever color you like—from a golden brown to black. When you're done roasting them, take them over to the table and lay them on half of a graham cracker. Put a chocolate bar on top of the marshmallows and top it off with the other half of your graham cracker. Then you kick back, relax, and enjoy every bite." When he was finished demonstrating, he licked the white marshmallow goo off his upper lip. "Got the idea, everyone? Come and get it!"

One thing he failed to mention was that skewers are not swords. A couple of the boys couldn't resist pretending they were acting out scenes from Pirates of the Caribbean, and started dueling. Mr. Dupries stepped in and stopped it before there was an emergency run to the nurse's station.

"But the skewers sound so cool clanking together," one boy told Mr. Dupries.

"Yeah, we were far enough apart so we didn't get hurt," the other added.

"In the dark, even pirates can get punctured. Go skewer a couple marshmallows and thrust them in the open-air oven. Do it, mateys, or you'll walk the plank," Mr. Dupries said playfully. He remembered what it was like to be a kid.

True to form, Ben left his marshmallows in the fire extra long until they were a nice golden black, as he liked to say. They caught fire so he blew it out and promptly assembled his s'more so the heat of the marshmallows would melt the candy bar. It was perfect. He inhaled the smell of melting hot chocolate and sweet burned sugar. A perfect bedtime snack.

About ten o'clock, the bugler played Taps again, signaling it was the end of the day—time to head for the tents. Ranger Moore blew his whistle and everyone became quiet.

"We've been having so much fun, I forgot to announce today's winner of our jacks and nine pins competition."

He walked over to the flagpole, which had a big spotlight shining on it, and picked up the trophy. Everyone followed him there and stood on their own side of the flagpole. The South wanted to keep the trophy, while the North wanted it to travel over to their side.

"When President Lincoln stood over there at the cemetery one hundred and fifty years ago, he began his speech by saying, "Four score and seven years ago, our fathers brought forth upon this continent, a new nation, conceived in liberty, and dedicated to the proposition that all men are created equal." Well, that must still be true because you are equal in your abilities, and equal in

your wins. Today, the North reigned supreme and this trophy will travel across the flagpole."

A roar of cheers erupted from the kids of New York, Pennsylvania, and Michigan. The others stood in silence—disappointed they had lost the competitions. However, just as the Northern players showed good sportsmanship yesterday, the Southerners did as well and formed a line to congratulate their opponents. Tomorrow would be the third and final day and the real winner would be announced.

Chapter 29

Back in their tent, Bekka and Hannah talked about the events of the day. Even though Stephen and Ben hadn't played jacks amazingly, their team had still won. But Hannah's thoughts were on her missing camera. The teachers had tried hard to find it, but the camera didn't show up. Bekka knew there had to be an explanation for what was happening, but she couldn't put her finger on it.

Lying in the dark on her cot, she again looked at pictures on the monitor of her camera. She was careful not to shriek when she saw those of the snake, taken right there by her cot where she was lying. Apparently the boys must have hidden the snake well out of sight as no one was talking about it. Maybe before they went home, she'd show it to Hannah and tell her it had been in their tent last night. She shuddered and hid her head inside her sleeping bag. It was just too much to think about it.

After taking a few breaths, she started looking at her pictures again, deciding which ones she wanted to print out. Suddenly, her hand stopped touching buttons on her camera. Her eyes bulged and just then, she almost jumped out of her skin like a snake. She'd figured out what was going on and had a pretty good idea how it was being done!

It was too late to go to the boys' tent, and she didn't dare walk over to Mr. Dupries' tent. She was sure nothing more was

going to happen tonight, so she lay there looking at the ceiling, devising a plan to trick the guilty party. First, she had to look up something in her Civil War information book. And it couldn't wait until morning!

Hannah was asleep so Bekka reached under her pillow, pulled out her flashlight and shined it under her cot until she found her information book. She searched for a certain chapter and reread something that happened during the Civil War. She was shocked to think it was happening right here under their noses and with the permission of Ranger Moore and his staff. She wondered if they had tried it before and no one had figured it out. She had to come up with a trap. She fell asleep with it on her mind and had dreams of being chased in and out of tents by people coming at her with snakes in their hands. She woke up in a sweat, relieved to know it was just a dream and not really happening.

Maybe she should become a detective rather than a nurse. Both jobs seemed rather exciting and risky. She lay there a long time plotting the plan that came to her mind. She determined it just might work. Finally, as the orange sky of sunrise was on the horizon, she fell into a deep sleep. This time without scary dreams.

Chapter 30

Right on schedule, the bugler played his wake-up song. Everyone met at the flagpole for the Pledge of Allegiance to the Flag before eating breakfast. Students from Pennsylvania and Virginia were in charge of making breakfast so learned to make starry-eyed eggs and toast. Mrs. Hopewell liked to do fun things with food, so introduced them to another new recipe.

"Anyone can fry or scramble an egg and make toast, but you're going to make a combo breakfast," she instructed. With a biscuit cutter, they cut circles out of bread and laid the slices of bread in a frying pan. Carefully, they broke an egg and poured it into the hole in the bread. After a minute, they flipped the whole slice over.

Morgan, Luke, and Sean from Pennsylvania got the hang of cracking eggs without breaking the yolks and had a pan of starry-eyed eggs ready when Mrs. Hopewell rang the triangle bell. The smells of a hot breakfast drifted over to the tents, making everyone come a running.

"Food, I just love food," Ethan told Ben and Stephen on the way over to the tables.

Ben nodded. "Me too. My dad says I'm on a "see-food" diet. I see food and I eat it. I keep telling him I'm a growing boy with a hollow leg."

They stood in line waiting to get their food at the buffet line. From way in the back of the crowd, Bekka called to Ben to save her and Hannah two seats at their table.

"I need to talk to you guys," she mouthed and did hand signals just so he knew what she was saying. Ben signaled okay with his head and reached for a tray.

Bekka was bursting at the seams to tell them about her discovery, but waited until the boys quit talking about how good the starry-eyed eggs and toast tasted. Finally, she got her chance to talk.

"I know who's doing it, and I know how it's being done!"

"You do?" Her brother almost choked on his mouthful of food.

"Yep, I figured it out last night when all of you were snoring your heads off."

"How'd you figure it out?" Ben asked, his eyes searching her face for a clue.

"Simple. With my camera."

"With your camera? Seriously? Did you catch the person red-handed?"

"No, but super-sleuth here read the facts in my book and put two and two together. We can't talk here because someone might hear us. When we're done eating, Stephen, get your metal detector and all of you meet me by the restroom entrance at the Visitor's Center. When I say something unusual, don't any of

you ask what I'm talking about. Just go along with me, okay? Act casual like we're talking right now."

What had Bekka discovered in a picture to make her come up with a plan like this? Ben, Stephen, Ethan, and Hannah were more than mystified at her plan, but Stephen trotted off to get his metal detector and met them at the entrance to the restroom area of the Visitor Center.

Bekka began talking in a bit of a loud voice. "Stephen, any hope of ever finding your jacks that came up missing from your tent?"

He raised his eyebrows and went along with her questioning. "No. I used my metal detector on practically every blade of grass and still can't find them anywhere."

"How about you, Ethan, did you find your jacks?"

"Nope, me neither." This conversation was blowing his brain. Not only did he not know what she was up to, but he also didn't have a clue as to who was supposed to be listening to them. Bekka had a pretty good idea the right people were hearing her.

Hannah jumped the gun and blurted out, "My camera is still missing, too!" Fortunately it sounded like a normal remark, so Bekka didn't ask her about finding the camera.

"I hope nothing else comes up missing. My grandpa would be really mad if his antique compass was stolen. He let me bring it in case we learned to use it on a hike in the woods. I'm leaving it in my tent so I don't drop it anywhere while we're playing games.

Oh yeah, that's right, it's time for us to get over there and play another new game."

She put her finger to her lips and signaled them to walk away with her. Stephen turned on his detector so no one would think they were acting suspicious. He still had hope that somehow, somewhere, his grandfather's ring would be found. But it seemed hopeless since it was the third and final day of their field trip in Gettysburg.

Once outside, Bekka smiled and high-fived them all. Her trap was set and they just had to wait.

Chapter 31

Ranger Moore had a funny smile on his face as he began instructions for the next event. "This morning's competition is back in the Visitor's Center and will be one which tests your memory and speed."

Kids looked at each other, shrugged their shoulders, and made grimacing faces. Some didn't want to think—they were on a field trip.

"Back in the 1860s, one way to send messages was using the telegraph. Any of you ever see one?"

Only a few raised their hands.

"President Lincoln wanted to make sure his messages got through to his generals in the Army, so he learned how to use the telegraph. Samuel Morse invented an alphabet code using dots and dashes. Each letter has a different number of them. Ever hear of the Morse code?"

Several raised their hands to that question.

"They also used the Railroad Morse code. Messages were sent through the telegraph wires which ran along the railroad lines. Wherever a railroad went, you could send and receive telegraph messages. In the American Morse code, an 'a' is a dot and a dash, a 'b' is a dash and three dots, and so on. Today, telegraphs have

been replaced with electronic keyers, which use the same dot and dash buttons to send messages.

"Once again, to give you a feel for being here at Gettysburg in July of 1863, this first game is a contest between states to send and receive a message using the American Morse code on an old telegraph."

"Sweet!" Ben declared. Being a Cub Scout, he already knew the Semaphore flags alphabet. He couldn't wait to tell Mr. Conroy, his scoutmaster, what he learned about the Morse code.

Ranger Moore continued, "In the recreation room in the Visitor's Center, you'll see a number of very old telegraphs. Beside them will be a stack of Morse code alphabet sheets. You will break into your small groups of ten and learn the alphabet enough to send and receive a message." He enjoyed watching their expressions at hearing this.

"It won't be just anyone out there waiting for your message. It's a clerk in the historical museum at your state capital, who's waiting for a specific message to be sent to him or her. You each have a different message on your paper, so don't copy anyone else's answer because it will be wrong. You'll send your message using only dots and dashes. Write them out first. It will help if you have your answer in front of you. It'll take a bit of time, but you can do it. Please notice, the papers are numbered in order. You must send your message in that order."

The looks of shock on their faces were worth taking a picture. This was something none of them expected to do, even in their wildest dreams.

"Teachers, get your students into their teams and let's get started. This should be a great learning experience."

Teams lined up and marched into the Visitor's Center, where Ranger Moore directed them to specific tables. Students hovered over their telegraphs to see how they worked. Ranger Moore blew his whistle to get their attention.

"Listen up! I'm going to demonstrate how this is done, so please watch carefully." It looked easy as he clicked out the words "President Lincoln" and then "it's as easy as pie".

"You have ten minutes to practice and then we'll send the official messages."

It seemed hard at first, but each student quickly learned how to do it and felt confident to form a word. No one could believe they were being allowed to use such important old machines.

"All right, teams, get a paper from the stack. The Morse code is at the top of the page. Your message is below it. When I give the signal, fill in your spaces and then in order, use the machine to send your message. Okay, on your mark, get set, go!"

Each student grabbed for a paper and got going. Some easily got the hang of deciphering the code, while others took a little longer. Before long, the clicking noises of the telegraphs were heard all around the room. Excitement mounted as dot and dash sentences were sent to historical museums in Atlanta, Columbia, Richmond, Harrisburg, Albany, and Lansing, where clerks were receiving the messages and answering back.

Soon the quieted machines began clicking again with a two-word answer. Ranger Moore told them not to reveal their response, so when it came through, it was written down and the papers were folded in half.

"Awesome. It's like the old-fashioned way of texting," Ashley from Virginia said, not believing she got a real answer. She'd never

been to the historical museum in Richmond so thought it was cool to communicate this way. She couldn't wait to tell her parents and would never forget her time in Gettysburg.

"I feel like I'm really living back then," Tyler from New York told his teammates. "It's like we could really get a message from the President or someone really important. I went to Albany once and saw the capital building, but didn't go to the historical museum, so I don't even know which building the clerk is in."

"It sounds like all the machines are quiet again," Ranger Moore said, observing each team with a folded paper in one member's hand. "Turn your papers in to your teacher for it to be scored. Your response will have the time you got the response stamped on it. That will count too."

Learning to use a telegraph had been a fun adventure, but while it was going on, Bekka couldn't help but wonder if there was any action going on over in her tent. She desperately wanted to look out a window! It might have been good if she had.

Chapter 32

"You do remember what we're looking for, right?"

"Yes, a compass. It's probably quite old and valuable if her grandfather gave it to her to bring."

"Yeah, that's why we're back over here. Keep looking in each tent until you spot it on the table. Just act normal."

"I'm trying to act normal, but I'm getting scared we're going to get caught."

"How can we? No one suspects us."

"Okay, you take those girls' tents and I'll do these. The one who did all the talking didn't have a Southern accent, so she has to be from the North."

They busied themselves searching each tent for a compass, spending as little time as possible in each one. Within five minutes, the compass was spotted and tucked away out of sight. She lifted up the flap and stepped out into the sunshine, a smile of sweet victory on her face.

As she came near her partner, she wordlessly nodded her head and kept going. These jobs were so easy. They could do this for a long time and get paid too. It was as easy as acting normal and neither felt sorry for those whose property they took.

Chapter 33

The students left the Visitor's Center to go eat a lunch of cold ham on homemade sandwich bread, pears, and oatmeal cookies. Ben was relieved the food still tasted good. He concluded they ate pretty good back in the 1860s. He needn't have worried over liking the food. Judging by the empty plates, the cooks scored a home run with this meal.

Ranger Moore stood up to speak. "While we set up for the last game, you'll have about an hour of free time. You may wander through the museum, work on your Junior Ranger books, find the monument dedicated to the soldiers from your state, or play one of the games you learned with a new friend. We hope you've made new friends from other states and have exchanged information so you can contact them after you go home. You are dismissed to go and have fun. The cannon will signal when it's time to begin the next competition."

Students scattered in all directions. Some went to play, some to hang out in their tents, some to work on their books, and some to explore. That would be Stephen and Ben. They wanted to explore the row of trees by the edge of the field one more time, looking for that impossible-to-find ring.

"If I don't find it there, I can at least tell my grandma I looked in every nook and cranny and open field we were in."

"Yeah, if it's still here, it's buried inches below the grass."

"And no one will ever own it again."

They were walking into their tent to get the metal detector when Bekka came bursting out of her tent. They let her come in.

With eyes practically bulging out of her head and her lips tight together, she collapsed on Ben's cot. "I know who's stealing the stuff and I know how they're doing it. I just have to prove it for sure!"

Hannah slipped into the tent behind Bekka, totally shocked her plan had worked. "She's awesome. And smart! I never would have figured it out."

"Who and how?" Ben demanded. "Don't just stand there, tell us."

"Scout's honor you won't tell anybody until we prove it?" She made her brother raise his first two fingers on his right hand like Cub Scouts do when they make a promise.

"Promise."

"You too, Stephen?"

"Promise."

Hannah didn't have to do it. Bekka trusted her not to spill the beans because she wanted to get her camera back.

"It was bugging me that things were taken and no one had them in their possession. When Evan had his lures stolen, I knew it couldn't be someone from the South wanting to make the North

lose. I knew there had to be a way of getting past everyone without being detected. So, I decided we should set up a trap this morning. In case you hadn't guessed, I left my old compass on my table. As you know, I had us talk about it down by the restroom so a certain person could hear us. Guess what's missing now? My compass! Bingo! I know who the culprit is. Look at my information book and look at my pictures here and here." She opened her book to the page that proved her suspicions. They were amazed and shocked to think they had played right into the thieves' plan.

"Wow," the boys said at the same time.

"You were so close, but didn't know it!"

"What are we going to do now?" her brother asked.

"You're going to act normal and not let on that you know anything. Got it?"

"Okay, but what if they suspect we know something? Do you think they might try to do anything to us?"

"Who knows? We don't know why they're stealing things. We just have to prove that they are."

Ben, Stephen, and Hannah sat and stared at Bekka. No one had any idea how to catch a thief red-handed.

"Well, until you decide what we should do," Ben concluded, "Stephen and I are going over by the trees to use the metal detector one last time. If you think of something, yell at us."

The boys reached under Stephen's cot, got the detector, and walked out into the afternoon sunshine. As they walked, they watched. Now that they knew who they were looking for, their eyes were open to how they could do it so easily.

Chapter 34

"Let's go back to the Nurse's Station and ask Mrs. Haynie if she'll finish showing us more things from the 1860s," Bekka suggested. "I think I might want to do a report on it when we get back to school. Maybe on the way over, I'll think of somehow to set another trap."

Hannah was filled with butterflies and looked in all directions to see if anyone was watching them. Not that she wanted someone to feel bad like she did at losing her camera, but she hoped someone else had something missing to help prove their point.

Mrs. Haynie was finishing up with a patient who had fallen and scraped her knee. "These long dresses can get in our way, can't they? Especially if you want to run. That's one reason very few women played sports back then. It was a long time before slacks were acceptable clothing for girls, but you can see what a good idea they would have been for horseback riding."

Bekka looked down at her long skirt. "Yeah, I'm glad I don't have to wear this all the time. I'm learning a lot about ladies and their dresses from back then. I bet you're glad you don't have to wear that long nurse's uniform all the time."

"Oh my, yes. I'd be tripping on something every day. Just a few minutes ago, I knocked over a tray of scissors, tweezers, and needles. I had to put them in the sterilizer again. I had just taken

them out of the cleaner from helping that lady with her nasty cut yesterday."

"Did she need stitches? Did you have to do them the old-fashioned way?"

"I cleaned it and gave her a couple stitches the normal way. I want it to heal without much of a scar. Her long dress will hide it for now, so no one will know she had an accident."

"If a person gets a snake bite, what would you do for them?"

Mrs. Haynie jerked her head and looked intently at Bekka and then at Hannah. Hannah wondered why Bekka would ask such a random question.

"Did you or someone else see a snake? The ranger warned me there are several kinds here in Gettysburg, but we are hoping with all this noise, they won't come around. Personally, they give me the creeps and I hope I don't have to deal with a snake bite; but if I do, I'll put my training into practice and act quickly. There's my snake-bite kit over there on the shelf, ready in case of an emergency. You do ask some good medical questions. If you keep it up, I think you will make a great nurse someday."

BOOM! The cannon went off signaling that it was time for the last game.

Bekka and Hannah thanked the nurse for the information and dashed out the door. Hannah thought they were going to play a game. Bekka intended to put her plan into action.

Stephen and Ben had been searching around a grove of trees without any success. When the cannon went off, they ran to the flagpole, taking the detector with them. Time was running out to discover any treasure at all.

Chapter 35

Over one hundred eager students, ready to start the last competition, surrounded Ranger Moore. He looked at the trophy on the North's side of the flagpole. Then he smiled at the players from the South.

"Is this trophy going to stay on this side of the flagpole?"

"No, sir!" they yelled back to him.

He turned to the players from the North. "Is this trophy going to stay on this side of the flagpole?"

"Yes!" The noise was deafening.

The ranger laughed at their reaction. He waved his hat to quiet them down. Both sides were convinced they were going to have the trophy on their side when the day was done.

"The final completion of the Games of Gettysburg will require a lot of footwork and agility. Men and women have always shown their speed through running. You'll all do well if you run fast, but you have to have a sharp eye as well. The last game is... Capture the Flag."

"All right!" Most of the boys felt confident they'd be good at it. They played Capture the Flag during gym at school and knew how to grab the flag without getting caught themselves. A number of girls jumped up and down because they were good at tag and

keep-away. At least they hoped they were fast enough to run away from the boys on the other side. They quieted down to listen to Ranger Moore finish speaking.

"During the Civil War, each side's flag was very important to the soldiers. Someone always held the battle flag and carried it out in front as they marched into battle. The South's Confederate flag was known as the Stars and Bars, while the Union flag was known as the Stars and Stripes. We want to be respectful of both flags, so we won't be using them in our game. We'll use handkerchiefs—red for the South and blue for the North." He held up one of each color for all to see.

"These are your flags. Each of you will get one from your teacher. Tuck it into your belt, waistband, or apron strings, and go stand on your team's white line and wait for my whistle. When you hear it blow, run toward your opponents and try to capture their flags. They can run away, but they can't hold on to their flag if you have hold of it. Once you get a flag, keep it, and go find another person on the opposite team who still has their flag. When your flag is taken, go sit on the ground behind your sidelines. The sound of my whistle will indicate the end of the game. Show your teachers how many flags you have in your hand and they'll add up the total of flags captured. We'll have three challenges. The winning team will be announced tonight. If no one has any questions, you can get your flags and go stand on your team's sideline."

It was chaos—everyone running to get their flags, finding a way to tuck them into their waistband tightly, and then getting to their sideline before the whistle blew.

Bekka had a dilemma. “How can I take pictures and keep my flag from being captured?” she asked Hannah. “I’ll want some, especially if we win. I guess I’ll have to take them after my flag is captured.”

“Be glad you still have your camera,” Hannah said while tucking her flag into her skirt’s waistband. “I wish I had mine. I sure wish I knew who took it.”

“Oh, we know who took it,” Bekka assured her. “We just have to figure out the best time to prove it.” She looked around for the guilty ones, but didn’t see them. “It makes you wonder if they think we are on to them.”

Just then, the sound of Ranger Moore’s shrill whistle filled the air, and the game was on! Noise and chaos was everywhere. Running, screaming, laughing, groaning, boys diving to the ground to escape being “captured,” and speedy kids out-running others. It was crazy—a good kind of crazy. Everyone was having the time of their lives with their new friends from the North and the South.

Bekka changed her mind about when to take a picture and in the split second it took to get a picture of Ben’s flag being captured, her flag was pulled away from her belt.

“Aw, I wanted to play longer,” she whined to Ben, walking to the sideline. To help herself feel better, she took pictures of others having their flag captured too. It happened to the best of them.

“Time’s up!” Ranger Moore yelled, blowing his whistle.

Kids with flags surrounded their teachers who frantically added up the score before the next challenge began. Two more times, each team ran as fast as they could trying to capture as many flags as they could before Ranger Moore blew his whistle. By the end of the competition, everyone's legs were exhausted. No one gave in easily because they wanted that traveling trophy at their school. Ranger Moore dismissed them while the teachers added up the points.

Ben and Bekka sat on the sidelines with their heads together. "What are we going to do if we don't have just the right chance to expose the thieves?" Ben asked.

Bekka's confidence came through loud and clear. "Oh, we'll come up with something. We still have a little time."

"I think we should take Stephen's metal detector with us wherever we go and when it goes off, we'll tell everyone what we know."

"I think you hit the jackpot, Ben. Let's do it and surprise everyone."

"I'll tell Stephen to keep it with him at all times."

When they stood up, Bekka put her hands on Ben's shoulders, looked him in the eye and said, "We'll be armed and dangerous in our own way."

"Let's go," Ben said and turned to find Stephen. Bekka made sure her camera was on so it was ready to catch any action when it happened.

Chapter 36

BOOM! The cannon went off for the last time. Everyone was to report to the flagpole for the big announcement of which team had won and then enjoy a celebration dinner.

If ever there was a blue ribbon given for a winning menu, Mrs. Hopewell would have won it for her roasted pig, corn on the cob, lettuce salad, and blueberry cobbler dinner. The smells drifted over to the game area, making students and adults alike wish they could eat dinner first.

"Anybody hungry?" Ranger Moore asked.

A chorus of "yes" and "yes, sir" rippled through the crowd.

"Hats off to the students from Pennsylvania and South Carolina who roasted a whole pig over an open fire. I hope it tastes as good as it smells."

Mrs. Hopewell approached Ranger Moore and talked quietly so no one could hear. He took out his pocket watch, checked the time, and lifted his clipboard.

Ben and Bekka searched the crowd for the suspected duo who'd kept out of sight pretty much all day. Stephen had his metal detector ready in case it looked like they had struck again.

"Mrs. Hopewell just informed me dinner is ready and will get cold if we wait for the trophy ceremony. We should have plenty of

time to announce the winners and hand out the awards after we eat." Cheering, clapping and whistles told the ranger, he had made the right call. "Once again, I believe it is fitting and in their best interest, for the ladies to go before the gentlemen."

The loudest groan ever was heard from the boys this time. It was in their best interest to have plenty of food—period! The smell was killing them!

"Don't worry boys, Mrs. Hopewell assured me it was a very large pig and the corn field is nearby, should we run out. All right girls, you may go first, but please remember there are sixty very hungry gentlemen ready to fight you for the last ear of corn."

Girls giggled as they lined up, some smirked at the boys who longed to get at the food. Being treated royally was fun.

Looking at his pocket watch one more time, Ranger Moore announced, "Be back here at six-thirty. One hour to eat is plenty of time. If you have a camera, bring it with you. Your families will want to see who won the trophy at the Games of Gettysburg."

While the girls made their way through the food line, Luke from Pennsylvania asked Ranger Moore how to tie a square knot on his blue Capture the Flag handkerchief. He wanted to use it as a scarf like soldiers used to do.

Ranger Moore set his clipboard, pen, and pocket watch on the trophy table and proceeded to show Luke how to do it. "Take your two ends in your hands. Just remember, it's right end over the left

one, then bring it up, and reverse it, left end over the right. Pull it tight and you have a square knot."

Others asked the ranger to do the same for them and before they knew it, the girls were served and it was their turn to eat. Ranger Moore tied scarf after scarf all the way to the food line.

Passing a table of girls, Ranger Moore stopped and asked, "Ever see a pig roasted like that before?"

"No," each one responded.

"It tastes super awesome," Taylor said, wiping barbeque sauce off her lips. "Is that how they cooked pigs back in the olden days?"

"Sometimes, when they had a big crowd of people to serve, but usually they cut it up into smaller sizes like we do now."

"I think my father should do this for our family reunion. My grandma would think it was the best meal ever." Ashley had a huge family, and her grandma Judy cooked food for days before their reunion.

Ranger Moore ate with the teachers, talking about the point totals and which side had won. They talked softly so students couldn't hear and spread which side had won. He asked Mrs. Ranes to add the final scores together again and then fold the paper.

The subject of the missing jacks, camera, knife, and fishing lures came up. No one had a suspect or a solution. The ranger offered to replace each item since no one could be accused of the

theft. He stood up to pull out his pocket watch to check the time, but it wasn't there. He remembered he'd left it on the clipboard sitting on the table when he tied the scarves for the boys.

"Anyone got the time? My pocket watch is over there on the trophy table."

Mr. Dupries turned his wrist around and checked his watch. "It's just about six-thirty. Time to get the show on the road."

Not having a microphone, Ranger Moore took a large pot and a pan cover and clanked them together. Kids put their hands over their ears.

"This is what they did before microphones were invented. It's a good way to get your attention. Did you get enough to eat?"

Once again, a chorus of 'yes,' and 'yes, sir' was heard from every direction.

"Good. Let's show our appreciation to Mrs. Hopewell for the great meals she and all of you prepared this week. Many of you came here never having cooked a meal and now you could go home and show your family how to cook food from the 1860s." Everyone clapped and banged on the tables. It was deafening, but genuine, because the food did taste good.

"Now, it's finally time for what you've all been waiting for—the trophy ceremony. Please head over to the flagpole and we'll begin immediately."

Little did he know the timing was off.

Chapter 37

Upon arrival at the flagpole, Ranger Moore took the paper from Mrs. Ranes with the point's total and put it on his clipboard. He put his pen in his shirt pocket and looked for his pocket watch. It was nowhere to be found! It was gone!

A huge lump formed in the ranger's throat. His watch, his irreplaceable watch, was missing. He could replace two sets of jacks, a camera, the Swiss army knife, and the fishing lures, but he couldn't replace his great-great-uncle's Civil War pocket watch which he had taken out of a safe at home to bring for the reenactment. This was the last straw! It was totally out of control!

He looked at the crowd of students who surrounded him. They looked like nice kids, not thieves. What was he going to do? Should he keep it to himself and quietly try to find who took it, or make a statement and search bags again? The problem was—no students had gone to their tents. They had all eaten.

He found Stephen and asked him to please use his metal detector around the flagpole and then walk over by the tables. Students watched wondering what was going on. Ranger Moore didn't explain. He wanted to make sure it hadn't dropped anywhere before he made a big deal of it being gone. Stephen's machine didn't indicate any metal was in the ground anywhere, making the ranger more disturbed. Finally, he got their attention.

"Boys and girls, listen up. You came to take part in a special Civil War reenactment here at Gettysburg. We intended it to be a fun week for all, but someone had other plans. It began with Stephen's jacks being taken, then Ethan's jacks, then Mr. Dupries' Swiss army knife, and Hannah's camera. We thought it was aimed at the Northern team, but then fishing lures were stolen from Evan on the Southern side. As bad as it seems to have all those things missing, I can replace them with new ones. Tonight during dinner, my great-great-uncle's Civil War pocket watch was stolen from off my clipboard. My watch is so old, it is irreplaceable. Before we can announce the winners, we must deal with the theft. I want all of you students to get in a line and empty your pockets before your teachers. And teachers, I want you to do the same in front of your students."

Shock and amazement showed on every face. Ranger Moore meant business in retrieving his stolen watch. Unfortunately for Ranger Moore, the contents of pockets were jacks, marbles, hair bands, and dirt when kids fell during Capture the Flag.

In a way, Ranger Moore was relieved to see that neither the students nor the teachers appeared to be guilty. He didn't want to, but he called in the rest of the staff. Mrs. Hopewell was clearing tables, but wiped her hands on her apron and came over; so did Mrs. Haynie who was heading for the Nurse's Station. The other rangers left their duties and came out, as did the laundry ladies who had collected the towels to wash them in the laundry area in the Visitor's Center. Each one was surprised they had to empty their pockets, but Ranger Moore wanted to be sure everyone was

proven innocent and no room was left for suspicion. All pockets and hats were turned inside out. Much to his dismay, Ranger Moore just looked at them all. "My watch could not vanish into thin air. It has to be somewhere on someone."

Ben, Bekka, Stephen, and Hannah were holding their breaths. They didn't want to blurt out anything until they were sure no one was proven to have stolen the watch.

Ben nudged Stephen to turn on his metal detector one more time and then walk over by the adults. Ranger Moore told him to turn it off because they had already searched the area. He obeyed, but Ben stepped forward.

"Ranger Moore, we have an idea who the guilty person or persons might be. All week, my friend Stephen, using his metal detector has been looking for his great-great-grandfather's ring, the jacks, Hannah's camera, Mr. Dupries' knife, and even the fishing lures, but we couldn't find any of them. Once in awhile it went off, but after lots of searching, nothing was found and the buzzing stopped. We couldn't figure it out; but then thanks to my sister's camera and a Civil War information book she's always reading, I think we know who took our things and how it was done."

Every single person surrounding the flagpole was shocked at the possibility of solving the mystery. Ranger Moore was beside himself wanting to know the truth.

"Who is it and how did you figure it out?"

Chapter 38

Ben took a deep breath before beginning the story. Either he would become a hero, or he would feel awfully foolish with this utterly shocking revelation.

"It started with Bekka taking a picture of the hoop petticoat under our principal, Mrs. Ranes' poofy dress. Sometimes, the metal detector would go off when we were by other ladies in their big dresses, and then it stopped when they walked away. Bekka read what happened during the Civil War and told us there might be a copycat crime here."

No one said a word. They just stared at Ben and listened.

"You see, during the Civil War, ladies sewed secret pockets into their petticoats and became spies in disguise for the army. They would hide maps, messages, knives, guns, and other things in their pockets when they came into camp, saying they were nurses or family members there to help with the sick. But really they weren't. Ranger Moore, if you would let Stephen turn on his metal detector and walk by the ladies over there, you just might find we have spies in disguise—not bringing things into our camp, but stealing them from the camp."

Ranger Moore's jaw dropped open and his eyes all but popped out of his head at this revelation. Wanting his watch back very badly, he told Stephen to turn it on and go over by the ladies.

A couple of them began to act awfully nervous when Stephen took a few steps toward them. As if on cue, the buzzing began, getting louder and going faster. Mrs. Hopewell and Mrs. Haynie had nothing to worry about as he approached them because they weren't guilty. Neither did the two rangers, whose pockets were still hanging inside out at their sides.

When Stephen got near the laundry ladies who had on their big wide skirts, it wouldn't quit. Metal was somewhere on them—but out of sight.

It would appear the guilty parties were busted! Stephen shut it off.

"We believe," Ben added, "they entered our tents undetected because they brought us pitchers of water and washcloths each day. But that was when the items were stolen. No one suspected they were the ones taking things left out on tables!"

"You might be onto something, Ben," Ranger Moore said, still hardly able to believe what was happening.

Rangers in uniforms went and stood behind the ladies in case they decided to run. Ranger Moore stepped in front of them and looked right into their faces. Every student held their breath. No one said a word except Ranger Moore.

"Mrs. Hopewell and Mrs. Haynie, please come and check inside these ladies' petticoats for pockets."

Mrs. Haynie was more than surprised to see she was facing Sonya Truce, whose leg had needed stitches the day before.

Reluctantly, she lifted Sonya's dress about six inches off the ground, showing her petticoat. Much to everyone's surprise, there were several small pockets sewn on top of the slip. Stephen's finger was still on the metal detector and it accidentally went off, buzzing like crazy. He quickly shut it off, but it let Ranger Moore know they were on the right track. Mrs. Haynie searched the pockets and in one of them, she found Ranger Moore's watch neatly tucked inside. As she lifted it out, her hand touched Sonya's leg.

"Ouch!" Sonya wailed.

Mrs. Haynie apologized for hurting her, but then a thought came to her mind. “You came to me with a nasty scratch and a cut yesterday. Did you get cut by a hook on a fishing lure?”

Many gasped hearing that accusation!

“No, and you can’t prove it,” Sonya nearly shouted, nervously looking at the other laundry lady, who immediately looked down at the ground. That was a clear indication of guilt!

Modern day spies in disguise!

Ranger Moore had never heard of such a thing, but here it was right before his eyes! He had Mrs. Hopewell check the other laundry lady’s petticoat. Sure enough, there were pockets, but nothing was in them.

Needing to get to the bottom of things, Ranger Moore instructed his rangers to take the women back to the laundry room in the Visitor’s Center and check their bags and sleeping area for the other missing items.

No one could believe the drama they were living through at Gettysburg. Where was a newspaper reporter when you needed one? Where were all the cameras? Everyone was too shocked to take a picture.

Chapter 39

Ranger Moore was speechless for almost two minutes while getting his composure. Several times he blinked his eyes and shook his head. Then he smiled a small smile, then a bigger one broke on his face, and finally he laughed and high-fived Ben, Bekka, Stephen, and Hannah.

A ripple of applause began somewhere in the crowd of fifth graders and teachers and soon it erupted into an amazingly loud continuous clap and cheer for the Fab Four from Michigan. They had saved the day for the Games at Gettysburg!

When the clapping had gone on long enough, Ranger Moore lifted his clipboard indicating he wanted to talk. It was time for the long-awaited announcement about the winning team.

"One hundred fifty years ago, there was a terrible three-day battle between states from the North and states from the South right here on these fields in Gettysburg. For the past three days, we have had terrific competition by students from states of the North and states of the South. The soldiers fought hard to win; you have played hard to win. You Southerners won two days ago, you Northerners won yesterday, and both sides tried hard to win today. I'm very pleased to announce..."

Ranger Moore stopped in mid-sentence, turning his attention toward the Visitor's Center. Voices and commotion came from that direction. The rangers were walking toward the crowd.

They had heard Ranger Moore's beginning statements, and one of them continued, "We are very pleased to announce… that Stephen, Ethan, Hannah, Evan and Mr. Dupries are the winners because we found each of their stolen items in an empty laundry detergent box hidden in a basket."

Hearing that announcement, eyebrows shot half way up most everyone's forehead. Clapping erupted again.

Pointing to Ben, Bekka, Stephen and Hannah, the ranger continued. "If it hadn't been for the keen eyes and quick thinking of these young people, no one, including you, Ranger Moore, would have gotten your things back. Those laundry ladies, our modern day spies in disguise, work for people who sell stolen property and you were easy targets. They practiced on the jacks and got braver taking the bigger items. Ranger Moore's watch would have gotten them a lot of money."

"Wow!" many of the students said, looking at each other. Ranger Moore couldn't believe what he was hearing. Ben, Bekka, Stephen, and Hannah were his heroes. This reenactment was one each of them would remember forever— not just for going to a famous historical place, but for stopping a ring of thieves.

The rangers handed everyone back their stolen items. Stephen and Ethan put their jacks in their pockets, Mr. Dupries did the same with his knife, Evan's teacher took the lures and Hannah started taking pictures immediately. Chaos broke out again with more clapping and high-fiving going on. Everyone was relieved the thieves had been caught before they headed home.

But the winning team still needed to be announced, and some wondered if it would it ever happen.

Chapter 40

Ranger Moore took charge of the situation and began his speech, his Gettysburg speech, which he had started and was interrupted when the rangers came with the stolen goods. He was determined to get through it and announce the winners once and for all. The crowd got quiet and listened.

He decided to be like President Lincoln and talk for only two minutes. He told them these games would long be remembered by those who participated, and he felt a valuable lesson had been learned. When things went wrong and doing the right thing was most important, everyone worked together for each other. And good came out in the end.

Before another interruption could happen, he lifted his clipboard and said with determination, "The moment we have all been waiting for. The moment we thought might not happen because of our spies in disguise. The moment of declaring a victor—or not." He dropped his voice and closed his eyes.

"What?"

"Say what?"

"No winner? What happened?"

More suspense. More drama. Students groaned. Waiting for the answer was too much.

"Your teachers assured me they kept accurate scores, reporting them just as you told them. We added and we re-added to be sure. You aren't going to believe it…"

He paused for effect—his head was bobbing up and down, his eyes wide open.

"Come on, we're dying of suspense," someone yelled.

"Drum roll, please," Ranger Moore called out.

Kids slapped their legs to make some noise.

"And the winner is... the South!"

Screams and hollers erupted from the South's side.

Ranger Moore had to yell above them. "And the winner is… the North!"

"What?" More screams and yelling.

"Yes, believe it or not, you tied."

Students couldn't help but stare at Ranger Moore and wonder how that could happen. He bent down, picked up the traveling trophy and declared, "You'll all be taking back a trophy to your schools." That news brought on even more yelling, clapping, and high-fiving.

Ranger Moore had everyone gather to pose for a large group picture which would appear in the Gettysburg newspaper and then he divided them into their state teams for more pictures.

Trophies were held high in each picture with smiling kids holding on to them.

After what they had just lived through, everyone was glad the teams had tied. They needed a happy ending. Those with missing things felt like the biggest winners because they had their stolen items returned.

Everyone wanted to have their picture taken with Ben, Bekka, Stephen, and Hannah—the Gettysburg heroes! What a newspaper story it would be when they got home.

When the crowd thinned out, the four of them walked back to their tents to pack their bags. Hannah's camera had one picture left to take before the memory card was full.

"I wish there was something special I could have my picture taken with that no one else has."

"Oh, yeah?" Ben asked. He and Stephen couldn't resist the first thing that popped into their heads. With a quick wink at his sister and a huge grin on his face, Ben said, "I think the perfect thing for you to pose with is in our tent."

"Really?" Hannah asked, looking at both boys.

"Yep, and you won't quit talking about it for a very long time."

And she didn't!

THE END

BEKKA'S F.Y.I. (For Your Information)

Gettysburg, Pennsylvania (PA) is 529 miles from Lansing, Michigan (MI)

Locate which direction the fifth graders' bus took them.

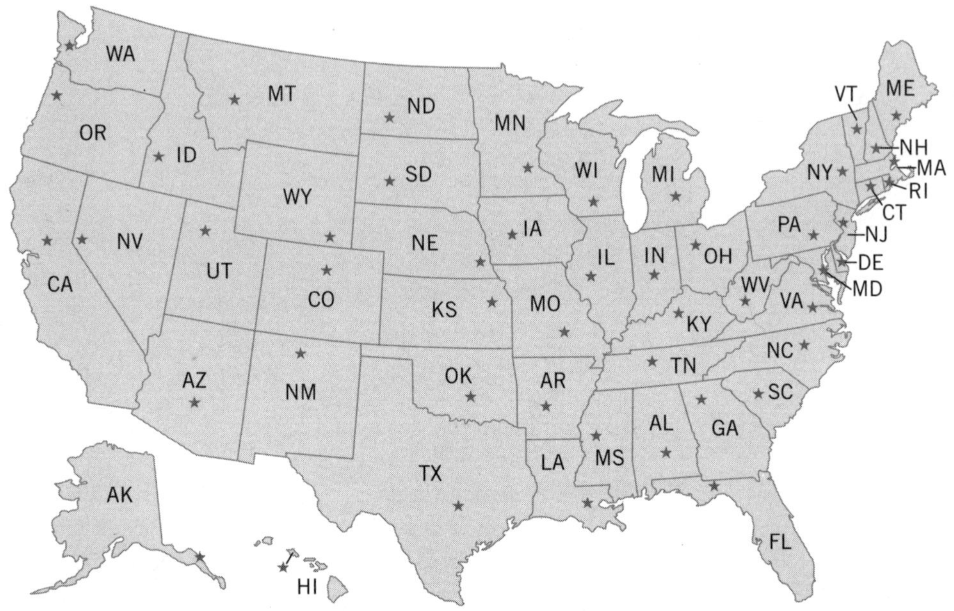

WHO, WHAT, WHEN, WHERE, AND WHY?

1. Why did Stephen say he wanted to go to Gettysburg?
2. Who was Bekka's tent mate?
3. What was the name of the competition between the North and South?
4. What did Stephen receive permission to take to Gettysburg?
5. Where were the pots of Mulligan stew put?
6. What was stolen from Mr. Dupries?
7. What did Bekka read while she was in Gettysburg?
8. Where did Mr. Dupries take Stephen and Ben to look for the ring?
9. What kind of snake was in the girls' tent?
10. What were spies in disguise?

Interesting facts about Pennsylvania:

1. Nickname: the Keystone State—In the early days of our country, Pennsylvania was the middle colony of the original thirteen colonies. It held the colonies together like the 'keystone' in a window or door arch.
2. Pennsylvania was settled in 1643. Philadelphia was the state capital during the Revolutionary War, and York was the first capital of the United States.
3. The state name meaning: Penn's Woods—after the father of Admiral William Penn, who the state was named for.
4. Capital city: Harrisburg
5. Important documents written in Pennsylvania:
   - The Constitution of the United States
   - The American Declaration of Independence
   - Lincoln's Gettysburg Address
6. State Flower: Mountain Laurel
7. State Tree: Hemlock
8. State Bird: Ruffled Grouse

FLAGS OF THE NORTH AND THE SOUTH DURING THE CIVIL WAR

North
Union Flag

South
Confederate Battle Flag

Interesting Facts About Gettysburg in 1863

1. 2,400 people lived in Gettysburg.
2. The battle at Gettysburg lasted three days—from July 1-3, 1863.
3. 170,000 troops from the North and South fought in Gettysburg; 51,000 were wounded, died, or went missing.
4. General Robert E. Lee was the commander of the Confederate Army of North Virginia.
5. Major General George G. Meade was assigned to be a commander of the Union Army of the Potomac just three days before the battle.
6. George Armstrong Custer (who later went to South Dakota near Mount Rushmore) led a Michigan cavalry brigade at Gettysburg, his first battle as a Brigadier General.
7. Brigadier General Elon Farnsworth fought with General Custer at Pickett's Charge and Little Round Top.
8. There were six famous battle locations: Seminary Ridge, Cemetery Hill, Culp's Hill, Devil's Den, Little Round Top, and Pickett's Charge. All of them are in the National Military Park.
9. Only one resident of Gettysburg was killed during the battle—Jennie Wade was accidentally shot by a stray bullet in her house.
10. President Lincoln gave his Gettysburg Address at the dedication of the Soldier's National Cemetery on November 19, 1863. It lasted only two minutes but was one of his most famous speeches.

George G. Meade
Commander of the Northern Army

Elon Farnsworth
from Michigan

Robert E. Lee
Commander of the Southern Army

President Lincoln's Gettysburg Address

November 19, 1863

"Four score and seven years ago, our fathers brought forth on this continent, a new nation, conceived in Liberty, and dedicated to the proposition that all men are created equal.

Now we are engaged in a great civil war, testing whether that nation, or any nation so conceived and so dedicated, can long endure. We are met on a great battlefield of that war. We have come to dedicate a portion of that field, as a final resting place for those who here gave their lives that that nation might live. It is altogether fitting and proper that we should do this.

But, in a larger sense, we cannot dedicate—we cannot consecrate—we cannot hallow—this ground. The brave men, living and dead, who struggled here have consecrated it, far above our power to add or detract. The world will little note, nor long remember what we say here, but it can never forget what they did here. It is for us the living, rather, to be dedicated here to the unfinished work which they who fought here have thus far so nobly advanced. It is rather for us to be here dedicated to the great task remaining before us—that from these honored dead we take increased devotion to that cause for which they gave the last full measure of devotion—that we here highly resolve that these dead shall not have died in vain—that this nation, under God, shall have a new birth of freedom—and that government of the people, by the people, for the people, shall not perish from the earth."

State Monuments

The Southern and Northern States in this story have monuments dedicated to those who fought at Gettysburg

A. NEW YORK
B. SOUTH CAROLINA
C. MICHIGAN
D. PENNSYLVANIA
E. GEORGIA
F. VIRGINIA

Camping Recipes

MULLIGAN STEW

Cut a small beef roast into bite size chunks.

Peel 6 carrots, 3 large potatoes, and 1 onion. Cut into small chunks.

Put the meat into the bottom of a large cooking pot.

Add vegetables on top.

Pour in 6 cups of water and 2 cups of tomato juice.

Add salt, pepper, and other seasonings to taste.

Cook in an oven for 2 hours at 350 degrees.

To make the broth into gravy, combine 3 Tablespoons of flour with 1/2 cup of water; mix well. Pour into pan and allow it to thicken the broth.

ENJOY IMMEDIATELY!

S'MORES

Place 2 marshmallows on a skewer and roast over a campfire.

When they are golden brown, remove and put on one half of a graham cracker.

Layer one half of a flat chocolate bar on top and add the other graham cracker.

ENJOY!

Morse Code

President Lincoln knew Morse Code and how to send telegrams.
Use the Morse Code to learn of Ben and Bekka's next National Park Adventure:

A	B	C	D	E	F
• —	— • • •	— • — •	— • •	•	• • — •
G	**H**	**I**	**J**	**K**	**L**
— — •	• • • •	• •	• — — —	— • —	• — • •
M	**N**	**O**	**P**	**Q**	**R**
— —	— •	— — —	• — — •	— — • —	• — •
S	**T**	**U**	**V**	**W**	**X**
• • •	—	• • —	• • • —	• — —	— • • —
Y	**Z**				
— • — —	— — • •				

__________   __________   ____________________

— • • •   •   — •   • —   — •   — • •   — • • •   •   — • —   — • —   • —

__________   ____________________

• —   • — •   •   — — •   — — —   • •   — •   — — •

__________   ______________   ________

— — —   • • —   —   • — — —   •   • • •   —   —   — — —

____

— • — —   •   • — • •   • — • •   — — —   • — —   • • •   —   — — —   — •   •

Meet the Characters

Real life twins, Hannah and Ethan, with their friend, Stephen holding a 4-foot snakeskin